TERENCE CONRAN'S

GARDEN
STYLE

TERENCE CONRAN'S GARDEN STYLE

CONSULTANT EDITORS
JOHN McGOWAN
AND ROGER DuBERN

PROJECT PHOTOGRAPHY BY
NADIA MACKENZIE

CROWN PUBLISHERS, INC.
NEW YORK

Originally published in Great Britain in 1991 by
Conran Octopus Limited
37 Shelton Street
London WC2H 9HN

Published by Crown Publishers, Inc.
201 East 50th Street
New York, New York 10022
Member of the Crown Publishing Group

Library of Congress Cataloging-in-Publication Data

Conran, Terence
     [Garden Style]
     Terence Conran's garden style / consultant editors, John McGowan
and Roger DuBern ; project photography by Nadia Mackenzie.
          p.   cm.
     Includes index.
     ISBN 0-517-58463-8 : $30.00
     1. Garden ornaments and furniture.   2. Garden Structures.
3. Gardens–Design.   I. McGowan, John.   II. DuBern, Roger.
III. Title.   IV. Title: Garden style.
SB473.5.C66   1991
717–dc20   90-21949
                                                                                        CIP

Printed and bound in Great Britain by Butler & Tanner Ltd,
Frome and London
Typeset by Servis Filmsetting Limited
Color separation by Chroma Graphics, Singapore

PUBLISHER'S ACKNOWLEDGMENTS
The publisher would like to thank the following for their invaluable assistance in producing this book:

Jonathan Chidsey, Lady Caroline Conran, Vana Hegarty, Gordon Hurden, Gareth Jones, Sian Jones, Wendy Jones, Harold Lee, Steve Stonebridge and everyone at Benchmark Woodworking Ltd, Hickson Timber Products Ltd, Bridget Bodoano and the Conran Shop, the Administrator of Castle Drogo and the National Trust

The projects in this book were specially built by SEAN SUTCLIFFE of Benchmark Woodworking Ltd

Special thanks to SIR TERENCE CONRAN for original project sketches and to PAUL BRYANT for his superb illustrations

Consultant Editors JOHN MCGOWAN and ROGER DUBERN
Project Editor JOANNA BRADSHAW
Editor SIMON WILLIS
Editorial Assistant ROD MACKENZIE
Contributor ELIZABETH WILHIDE
Americanizer RAY PORFILIO

Art Editors HELEN LEWIS, MERYL LLOYD
Illustrator PAUL BRYANT
Visualizer JEAN MORLEY

Photographer NADIA MACKENZIE
Photographic Assistant SIMON ANDERS

Production Manager SONYA SIBBONS
Picture Research NADINE BAZAR

SPECIAL NOTE
Before embarking on any of the projects in this book, you must check the law concerning building regulations and planning. It is also important to obtain specialist advice on plumbing and electricity before attempting any alterations to these services yourself.
   Whilst every effort has been made to ensure that all the information contained in this book is correct, the publishers cannot be held responsible for any loss, damage, or injury caused by reliance upon the accuracy of such information.

DIMENSIONS
Do not mix metric and imperial dimensions when you are making a calculation.

CONTENTS

INTRODUCTION

If you have a garden, the chances are that you already "do it yourself." Planting, seeding, mowing, turfing, fencing, and paving are tasks that the majority of gardeners do themselves, since few people today have either the space or the means to justify a full-time gardener.

This book is a logical extension of that established tradition of working outdoors in the garden. It contains a range of projects, from the simple to the more complicated, and shows you how to make a variety of structures, including containers, seats, trelliswork, and even a summer house. All of these are classic garden accessories, the design of which is too often overlooked.

Achieving success with these projects has to do with confidence. Once you have completed a simple project, this will give you the confidence to move on to a more complicated piece. If you are a novice woodworker, choose the simplest item in terms of design and progress gradually as your skills and dexterity develop.

If the garden is a good place to practice and refine your remodeling skills, you can also get away with a lower standard of finish: precision and perfection are not really at home in the garden, where a weathered, rustic appearance can be a positive attribute. Materials need not be expensive and what you make will usually have cost less than the retail

product in the garden center, although this is not invariably the case. You can buy lattice, for example, for far less than the wood you would need to make it, so to economize by doing-it-yourself you must examine what is commercially available from the garden center and make the proper comparisons.

The great benefit of building things for the garden, however, is the degree of satisfaction it affords – the pleasure of making something that has been tailored to suit your own space and needs. What you make will often be better designed than its equivalent in the garden center; more importantly, it will reflect your own taste and sense of style.

Terence Conran.

PLANNING A GARDEN

In the words of Sir John Soane, good design should contain an element of "hazard and surprise." Although Soane was talking about interior design, this important principle applies equally to the disposition and arrangement of outdoor space. Nothing is less memorable than a garden which can be surveyed in a single glance: you want to be able to move through a garden and be surprised by what you discover around each corner.

Fortunately, "hazard" in gardening is easy to create. Changes of direction, with paths leading around structures which divide and separate different areas within the garden, immediately generate interest. Forms can be created very simply with trelliswork over which climbing plants are trained, providing a sort of growing "veil" through which to walk.

Even more important are changes in level. In this, as in so much of garden design, there is a great deal to be learned from Japan. Different levels give a sense of movement, transforming even the dullest

patch of ground. And because plants like falling over edges or trailing over walls, a change in level provides endless opportunities to blend architectural form with planting, thereby softening the lines of the design.

Trellising, planters adjacent to the house, fast-growing creepers and climbers grown up the walls can all help to blend a house in with its setting, anchoring it to its environment and creating an established garden within a short space of time. One great advantage of building garden accessories is that if your house has distinctive architectural details, such as decorative bargeboarding, it is easy to incorporate these features into the design of your structures. Something as simple as picking out a color from a door to use on seating or containers can help to unify the overall design and visually link the house to the garden.

Because the garden is an organic place where things grow, the materials you use for structures and accessories should be

natural ones as far as possible. Plastic has no affinity with plants: the two simply do not go together. Artificial materials always stand out in a garden because they do not weather in the way that natural ones do. Wood, stone, terracotta, brick, and – for some reason – metal all work well in the garden, harmonizing with one another so that you can vary the textures and surfaces in an interesting way. What is particularly appealing about all of these materials is the way they age and weather, oxodizing, bleaching, staining, and acquiring lichens and mosses so that they meld into the garden. Show gardens, because they have not had time to mature, always look too new and clean for my taste. You can encourage aging if your garden is looking too new by scrubbing salt or domestic bleach into wooden decking to achieve a weathered look or by painting non-pasteurized milk, house-plant food, or manure made into a slurry onto concrete or terracotta surfaces to speed up the growth of lichen.

THE OUTDOOR ROOM

Good garden design is a question of creating an outdoor space that reflects your needs, style, and preferences, and is at the same time compatible with the materials, structures, and details of your house. The garden should be a natural extension to the house, rather than a jarring contrast. Sources of inspiration for garden designs include the ever-popular informal look of the English country cottage, the architectural terraces of modern urban gardens, and the contemplative beauty of Japanese landscape settings.

If the garden needs an element of wilderness and a certain lack of precision to be truly inviting, it is also the place for color. Far too often, people play safe with garden accessories, sticking to the traditional shades of white or a dark green which fades into the background. Splashes of bright color are an attractive and appealing feature of Mediterranean gardens and, contrary to popular belief, such vivid accent shades also work in countries where summer light is not as intense. Color makes a strong positive statement, and is also extremely cheerful in the winter when the garden is least interesting. Yellow, for example, goes equally well with the fresh greens of summer and the grays of winter. Blue (either dark blue or blue-gray) is another good garden color. If you make your own garden accessories, you can decide for yourself what color you want to paint them, rather than having to accept the limited and uninspiring shades that are offered commercially.

Finally, a garden, in the same way as a room, needs a focus of interest: the path must lead somewhere; the view through the pergola must reveal something at the other end; a formal layout of beds demands a centerpiece. Whatever you base your design around should look positive and well-considered, not half-hearted. A large terracotta pot tumbling with colorful plants, an inviting garden seat in a shady place, a patio under a striped awning, a garden pond full of fish or a collection of strange, disparate containers all make good focal points as long as they are properly complemented by their environment. There are many excellent ideas illustrated in this book to stimulate your imagination, but the important point is that these are merely a starting place for your own plans and ideas. Your garden is the place where you can express your own personality and idiosyncracies to create the kind of outdoor room you want to live in, whether it is formal or rustic.

PRACTICALITIES

A new garden should start with a plan which takes into account practical as well as aesthetic considerations. A camera is a useful tool in the planning process: take photographs of the views from the house to the garden (and from upper levels, too) as well as from the garden to the house. A simple sketch of the plot annotated with rough dimensions will help you to decide on the layout of paths, beds, and patio. For a formal design you may wish to work out a strong controlled grid or a symmetrical framework of beds and connecting paths. For a more informal, natural arrangement, it is still important to think about where the paths will go and what shape beds they will create: too often, paths are laid without due regard to the shape of the beds, with awkward and ill-judged results. You should also work out any changes in level required or note existing slopes or steps, as well as features such as mature trees and garden sheds.

PLANNING A GARDEN

Although the climate of your garden cannot be altered radically, it can be tempered. Exposure to strong winds can be limited to some extent by the filtering effect of boundary hedging, fencing, or trellis. In a dry area, a damp microclimate can be created by the addition of a pond, around the perimeter of which moisture-loving plants can flourish. Shade can be supplied by a variety of means, both manmade and natural, including awnings, arbors, and vines or climbers trained over trellis or wire frameworks. Too little light poses another problem. You cannot, of course, reorientate a garden which faces the wrong way, nor do much about the deep shade cast by high walls. But you can clear out overgrowth, take down fencing, and drastically prune overhanging branches to let in as much light as possible. Unfortunately if the sun doesn't shine, there is little you can do about it.

Many other factors will have a bearing on the eventual design:
● The siting of a compost heap, a tool shed, and utility area
● Access to water
● The position of eating or sitting areas
● Barbecues
● Areas in which children can play and in which to site play equipment
● Permanent fixtures such as mature trees, existing walls, and boundaries
● The presence of any eyesores which may need to be camouflaged
● The need for privacy or security
● Noise from neighboring gardens
● Special requirements such as the extreme climate of a roof garden
● The amount of time you can spend
● Your budget

All gardens benefit from careful organization. Planting stands a greater chance of success if the basic framework is right.

DESIGN AND DETAIL

Gardens thrive on an element of surprise, hidden corners, and changes of level. Decking is a harmonious outdoor surface, and can be planned in advance to provide different seating and eating levels, and beds for planting (above). Strategically placed, arbors or trelliswork can act as a focal point in the garden, directing the eye to splashes of color (above left and opposite).

COLOR IN THE GARDEN

Color has long been a neglected element in the garden as far as structures, accessories, and garden furniture are concerned (overleaf). Containers, seats, trellises, fences, and walls can all be painted to give a positive lift to the overall design of a garden.

PART 1

SEATING AND EATING

In every garden there should be a place where you can sit down, look with pleasure at what you have achieved, and think about all the hard work that remains to be done. Any seating area, whether it is a bench in a shady corner or a patio equipped with table, chairs, awning, and barbecue, becomes a focal point in the garden's design; its position, accordingly, is part of that initial process of architectural planning. Should it be in sun or shade? In view of the house or in a more secluded location? If you intend to eat outdoors, at least partial shade will be required. Eating outside, preferably in dappled sunlight, is one of the great pleasures of life.

You can sit in the garden to read a book, have a drink, watch the children play, eat a meal, or simply take stock of your surroundings, and there are as many styles of garden seat as there are functions for them to fulfil. Which type of seat you choose should reflect the general plan and style of your garden. The quality of light and shade is a very important consideration, not only for personal comfort, but also for good growing conditions and for intrinsic interest.

SEATING AND EATING

Seats and table tops must be designed so that water does not sit on the surface and rot or rust them away. A fractional tilt to a seat or table top will ensure that water drains off; slats or drainage holes fulfil the same function and there are also new outdoor paints which protect garden furniture to a much greater degree than traditional undercoat and gloss.

Much garden furniture, particularly the cast-iron or painted metal variety, is too ornate for my taste. Tables and seats which are clean-lined, whether they are curved or rectilinear, look more confident and suit outdoor living much better. Simple garden furniture allows the focus of attention to remain on the planting. This is not to dismiss wrought-ironwork entirely. Benches with wrought- or cast-iron ends, but plain slatted backs and seats, can be attractive and are more comfortable than all-metal versions which heat up in the sun.

Garden seats can also be amusing. In the nineteenth century, rough-hewn tree branches were nailed together to create whimsical Gothic benches, a kind of visual joke. In a similar vein are sections of tree trunk used as bench supports, a chimney pot filled with sand as a table base, or a stone slab inset into a clipped box hedge, with the foliage making a living upholstered back. One of the most irresistible designs is the tree seat, almost a ground-level tree house, which forms a platform around the base of a tree.

In addition to semipermanent garden furniture, there are many varieties of ready-made garden seating which work equally well indoors. Painted wooden benches, wickerwork, rattan and basket chairs, folding canvas chairs, and metal park chairs suit their location and are generally light enough to move easily.

With garden tables, there is the same choice between permanent fixtures and tables which can be set up as required. Stone, marble, and ceramic tiles are excellent materials for table tops; folding

OUTDOOR LIVING

Stepped wooden seating (above) provides interesting and versatile changes of level in a garden. A terrace of herringbone paving and shaded by mature plane trees (right) makes a delightful outdoor eating area.

Overleaf A range of garden seating ideas.

SEATING AND EATING

metal tables, traditionally associated with French parks are more economic.

Seating areas are almost always more pleasurable and useable if there is a degree of shade. If your patio is exposed to the full force of the sun, there are many ways of creating shade that look appropriate as well as stylish. In this area, the yachting world is a fruitful source of visual ideas. Sail-like canvas awnings, varnished wooden frameworks for climbing plants, and canvas in bright clear colors eyeletted and lashed to a simple metal frame all have a faintly nautical flavour. A simple metal armature or framework with a vine trained over it is a particularly Mediterranean solution to the problem; narrow gauge trellis overhead breaks up sunlight into a small square grid, taking the power out of it. Shop blinds fitted with a retractable mechanism, canvas clipped on to a wood and wire frame, or a large market umbrella are other effective ideas. For a more theatrical effect, a bright, patterned fabric can be knotted and tied to poles like an oversize scarf, or you can borrow ideas from tent design. Plain canvas (perhaps painted on the underside) or broad blue-and-white stripes are crisp, fresh, and appealing.

Most people today want their outdoor eating area to be a cooking area as well. A barbecue area is particularly easy to build, a good project to build in the garden. Brick or stone are the best materials for construction and you will probably also need to pave around and beneath the barbecue to make cleaning easy. At the simplest level of design, you can buy a mass-produced, cast-iron barbecue and simply set it on a brick or stone slab. If you are building the barbecue as well as its setting, it is best to line it in firebrick as a precaution against the intense heat.

Barbecues should be sited with care. Not only do they generate a great deal of heat, they are also smoky. Avoid positions where smoke and cooking smells will drift into the house – or worse, through your neighbor's windows. Overhanging plants are likely to be singed or even incinerated; adjacent walls will be blackened by smoke, although this is not necessarily unattractive.

You can extend the potential of out-door eating areas by the addition of good garden lighting. Outdoor lighting calls for a degree of sensitivity, since obvious, glaring fixtures will immediately rob your garden of whatever charm it possesses; on the other hand, subtle, diffused light sources create an instantly magical atmosphere. Garden lighting should be as unobtrusive as possible, with fixtures built into walls or shielded in some way.

When you furnish a garden, what you choose should be simple, so as not to compete with the planting; practical, for obvious reasons; and architectural, to contribute to your overall plan or design. You can use this opportunity to go one step further and think about the way you furnish your home indoors as well: a continuation of the same basic attitude will bring the house and garden closer together, to the benefit of both.

OUTDOOR SEATING AREAS

If you intend to use a seating area as a place for outdoor meals you will need to provide a degree of shade or shelter. Sitting in the full glare of the hot midday sun is very unpleasant for any length of time; on the other hand, you do not necessarily want to have to move indoors on account of a few drops of rain. Solutions include integrated terraces and balconies, awnings, and trellises supporting a canopy of vines or climbing plants. Perhaps the most appealing of all in fine weather is a table and chairs placed in the dappled shade under a tree, a natural shelter which filters the light to just the right degree.

GARDEN BENCH

When it comes to garden furniture, people tend to have rather conservative taste. Although they might tolerate modern and even occasionally avant-garde pieces in the home, these are less welcome for outdoor living, where the emphasis has generally been on the traditional. Wrought-iron seating typically has a Victorian flavor, and, in recent years, the designs of Sir Edwin Lutyens have been enormously influential, with their classically inspired curves.

This garden bench with its upright railed back and plain, flat seat and legs owes something to the strict functional beauty of nineteenth-century Shaker furniture. Extremely simple by comparison with much of what is commercially available for the garden, the bench is nevertheless one of the more demanding projects to make. This is partly because garden furniture must be finished to a higher standard than other garden structures, as it will receive closer inspection.

Even if you move your garden furniture indoors for the winter it will have to take some degree of weathering. Allowing water to collect on a surface is the quickest way of causing deterioration and decay. Here the seat slopes slightly so that water drains off and, similarly, where the back joins the seat a narrow gap has been left to allow water to flow down. The straight edges of the legs are beveled so that accidental knocks by the lawnmower do not cause too much damage.

The height of the back is a critical factor in the design. Equally distinctive is the back's reeded quality. This is, perhaps, not a bench for lounging, although, supplied with a long cushion, it would work very well indoors.

Don't be afraid to let color make a positive statement in the garden. Yellow and various tones of blue look as good in winter as they do in summer and are more eye-catching than the more sedate shades of dark green or white.

GARDEN BENCH

The garden bench is perhaps the most familiar piece of garden furniture. Building one yourself will almost certainly be cheaper than buying one, and will give you a real sense of satisfaction. If need be, you can adapt the design shown here to suit the size and proportions of your garden and your individual requirements. Choose the site for your bench with care, positioning it to serve as a focal point that draws the eye in a certain direction; alternatively, you could place it to provide a place of sanctuary in a tranquil, shady corner of the garden where you can retreat to sit in peace, quiet, and comfort.

This garden bench could be made from hardwood, but it will be considerably cheaper and more environmentally acceptable if you make it from good-quality softwood. In the latter case, it is important that you treat the lumber with good-quality wood preservative at all stages of construction to ensure that it will give you many years of service. A clear wood preservative should be applied to the lumber after the component pieces have been cut, but before the joints are assembled; the strength of the joint will not be affected if you allow about 24 hours for the preservative to dry thoroughly before applying the glue. A second coat of preservative should be applied after construction, before the application of the final finish.

Using clear preservative will allow you to keep your options open regarding whether you finish the bench by painting or by applying a water-repellent wood stain of the type used widely on wood window frames. If you finish the bench by painting it, it is a good idea to use an exterior gloss paint or microporous (satin sheen) system. Such paint often contains a penetrating preservative wood primer, and this should be used in preference to a second coat of clear wood preservative.

The ideal way to construct the bench to ensure many years of service is to use traditional mortise and tenon joints for the main frame and dowel joints for the back rest slats and the seat boards. However, if you feel that you do not possess the necessary skills to cut accurate mortise and tenon joints, then the entire bench could be made using dowel joints throughout. If you do use only dowel joints, however, it will be more important than ever to apply a good-quality waterproof woodworking adhesive to each joint before assembly, and to keep each joint firmly clamped until the adhesive is thoroughly set.

MATERIALS

Part	Quantity	Material	Length
BACK LEGS	2	3 × 4in (75 × 100mm) S4S softwood	41in (1035mm)
FRONT LEGS	2	3 × 3in (75 × 75mm) S4S softwood	17in (430mm)*
SIDE FRAME RAILS	4	2 × 3in (50 × 75mm) S4S softwood	19in (480mm)
FRONT RAIL	1	As above	70½in (1790mm)
LOWER BACK RAIL	1	1¼ × 6in (32 × 150mm) S4S softwood	70½in (1790mm)
UPPER BACK RAIL	1	2 × 3in (50 × 75mm) S4S softwood	74in (1880mm)*
BACK SLATS	32	1 × 1½in (25 × 38mm) S4S softwood	Distance between back rails
SEAT BOARDS	4	1¼ × 6in (32 × 150mm) S4S softwood	73¼in (1865mm)
DOWELS (seat to lower back rail)	5	From ½in (12mm) hardwood doweling	Approx. 3¾in (95mm)
DOWELS (to join seat boards and fit back slats)	As required	From 5⁄16in (8mm) hardwood doweling	Approx. 1½in (40mm)

* Overlong and then cut to size after affixing – see text

TOOLS

WORKBENCH (fixed or portable)

UTILITY KNIFE

STEEL MEASURING TAPE

STEEL BENCH RULE

TRY SQUARE

SMALL CROSSCUT SAW (or circular power saw)

BACK SAW (or power saber saw)

CHISELS

MARKING GAUGE

MORTISE GAUGE

POWER DRILL

BRAD-POINT DRILL BIT – (5⁄16in) 8mm

SPADE BIT

DOWELING JIG

ONE PAIR OF BAR CLAMPS (or band clamp)

SMOOTHING PLANE

POWER ROUTER and BEADING BIT

MALLET

ORBITAL SANDER (or hand sanding block)

GARDEN BENCH ASSEMBLY

BACK LEG

BACK SLAT

DOWELS

SEAT BOARD

FRONT LEG

FRONT RAIL

UPPER BACK RAIL

LOWER BACK RAIL

TOP SIDE FRAME RAIL

LOWER SIDE FRAME RAIL

BACK LEG

SEAT BOARDS

TOP SIDE FRAME RAIL

FRONT LEG

LOWER SIDE FRAME RAIL

SIDE ELEVATION

GARDEN BENCH

1 **Shaping the Back Legs**
Lay front leg at an angle on back leg and mark its position. Measure 1⅜in (35mm) from the back at the top and join marks with top of front leg marks. Cut out around marked lines, curving the shape at the back. Mark off seat thickness parallel with top of front leg position.

SEAT SIDE FRAMES

SHAPING THE FRONT LEGS

Cut the front legs overlong – at least 17in (430mm) long in total – and measure 15¾in (400mm) up from the bottom to mark off the finished length. Square a line around the leg on all faces (see **Techniques, page 148**). Put the front legs aside for the time being.

SHAPING THE BACK LEGS

The back legs are shaped from 3 × 4in (75 × 100mm) lumber. Mark out the legs by laying one of the front legs on the wider face of one of the back legs, sloping at an angle but touching at the bottom and side edges (fig. 1). Remember that the front leg is overlong at the top, so align with the finished leg line. Mark around the shape of the front leg onto the back leg.

At the top of the back leg, measure 1⅜in (38mm) from the back face on both sides and join these two points to the top points of the marked front leg position, giving the shape for the back leg (fig. 1).

With one back leg marked, cut out around the marked lines, with straight lines at the front face of the leg, but rounding off the angle at the back of the leg to produce a gentle curve. Plane the face edges at the front straight and square to the sides as the joints are measured from this edge.

Use the cut-out back leg to mark the other one and cut it out. When both legs are cut, mark off the seat thickness, parallel with the top of the front leg position, using a seat board and a try square.

MARKING UP THE MORTISES AND TENONS

Take one of the front legs and line one of the side rails (wide face against the leg) to the top marked line (fig. 2), taking into account the excess length at the top. Mark off the position of the bottom of the rail onto the leg. Working from this line, mark off the length of the mortise 2in (50mm) up. Square the lines around to the two inside faces *(see* **Techniques, page 148***)*.

For the bottom joint, measure 2⅜in (60mm) up from the bottom of the leg on the back face, then another 2in (50mm) up for the top of the mortise. Transfer all of these lines to the back of the other front leg using a try square. Square the lines of the top mortise around to the inside face of the second front leg.

Using a try square, transfer the length and position of the mortises from the front legs onto the front face of the back legs.

Take a ¾in (19mm) chisel and set a mortise gauge to this width with the stock set so that the mortise is centered on the edge of the side rails (*not* centered on the legs).

Mark off the top mortises on the front faces of the back legs, and on the two inside faces of the front legs. Measure from the *outside* edge in each case so that the front and upper side rails will be flush.

On the ends of all four side rails, mark off the tenons (fig. 3) and also mark off the tenons on the ends of the front rail.

Re-set the stock on the mortise gauge so that it is centered on the legs and mark off the lower mortises centered on the inside faces of all the legs for the lower side rails.

Measure 2in (50mm) in from each end on one of the side rails, and mark the shoulder of the tenon. Square around all faces. Using a try square, transfer the lines onto all the other side rails. Measure 2in (50mm) in from each end of the front rail and square around as before. To ensure a strong construction, it is important that all the lengths between the shoulders on the side rails are accurately marked. Mark the widths of the top tenon 2in (50mm) from the bottom edges of all the *top* rails so that the tenons are bare-faced to the lower edge.

The tenons are centered on the two *lower* side rails, so measure ⅜in (10mm) up from the lower edge, then 2in (50mm) for the width of the mortise (fig. 3).

CUTTING THE JOINTS

Cut the mortises slightly deeper than 2in (50mm) *(see* **Techniques, Mortise and Tenon Joint, page 154***)* and then the tenons.

Dry assemble the parts to check the fit. The ends of the tenons on the front rail and the ends of the front tenons of the top side rails will all need to be cut at a 45° angle to ensure a tight fit (fig. 4).

Cut off the "horns" (protruding ends) at the tops of the front legs to leave the front legs flush with the upper side rails.

THE BACK

FITTING THE LOWER BACK RAIL

Take a chisel about ½in (12mm) wide and set a mortise gauge to exactly this width. Set the stock so the tenon will be offset to the back on the lower back rail, making a bare-faced tenon joint (fig 1., page 28). Mark the mortise on the inside faces of the back legs, working from

the front faces. Mark the bare-faced tenons on the lower back rail.

Align the lower back rail with the mark for the seat at the front so that it is square to the top front face of the back leg (fig. 1, page 28). Mark off the position of the rail, and mark a ⅝in (15mm) shoulder at the top and bottom.

On the lower back rail, mark 2in (50mm) in from the ends and ⅝in (15mm) in from the edges for the shoulders. Before cutting the tenons, check that the length between the shoulders is the same as the front rail. Cut the tenons and then chisel the mortises to a depth of 2in (50mm).

FITTING THE UPPER BACK RAIL

Mark 2in (50mm) down from the top of the back leg and square around using a try square. Transfer these lines to the other leg. With the mortise gauge still set to ½in (12mm) set the stock so that it is centered on this shoulder line, working from the front face (fig. 2, page 28). Now mark off the tenon on both legs.

② **Front Leg Mortises**
Mark rail positions on leg. Mortise centered on edge of front and top side rails, centered on lower side rail.

③ **Front and Side Rail Tenons**
Top **Cut bare-faced tenons for front and top side rails.** *Bottom* **Tenon is centered on lower side rail.**

④ **Dry Assembly of Front Legs to Front and Side Rails**
Left **Position of cut mortises on front leg.** *Inset* **Plan view shows front rail and upper side rail flush with outside edges of front leg.** *Right* **Ends of tenons are angled on front and upper side rails.**

Garden Bench

The upper rail should be cut over-long by 2in (50mm), but use the lower rail to mark the exact length between the shoulders and square around the upper rail at each end. From these lines mark 2in (50mm) to the outside (toward the ends).

With the mortise gauge still set for the width of the tenon, mark the mortises on the bottom edge of the rail, working from the front face (fig. 2). Mark the width of each tenon to 2in (50mm) from the inside face of the legs so that the tenons are bare-faced.

Cut the mortises to 2in (50mm) deep, and cut the tenons. Dry assemble the back legs to the upper and lower rails to check the fit and cut off the "horns" (protruding ends) flush with the outer face of the legs.

Shaping the Upper Rail

The upper rail has to be shaped at the back to follow the taper of the back legs (fig. 3). Strike a line up each back leg to continue the taper onto the rail and then join up these lines by marking a line along the top edge of the upper rail.

Remove the rail and cut off the waste with a power plane or by using a crosscut saw. This is a long rip cut and will need care. Finish the taper by planing the surface of the upper rail smooth.

Fitting the Back Slats

The width and spacing of the back slats are matters of preference. We used 1 × 1½in (25 × 38mm) slats, spaced about ¾in (19mm) apart.

The easiest way to fit the slats is to use two dowels top and bottom, positioned by means of a doweling jig. We used $\frac{5}{16}$in (8mm) dowels, 1½in (40mm) long. For an even stronger fitting you can use mortise and tenon joints top and bottom, but without a mortising machine it would be a very time-consuming task to make all the necessary joints.

Measure on the back leg the distance from the top of the lower rail to the underside of the upper rail, and cut the slats to this length if you will be affixing them using dowels. Cut the slats about ¾in (19mm) longer at each end if you intend to use mortise and tenon joints.

Detail of the Garden Bench
For decorative effect, the outside edges of the legs, frame rails, seat boards, and so on are beveled before final assembly.

① Fitting Lower Back Rail to Back Leg
Lower back rail fits square and flush with slope of front face of back leg and will align with back edge of seat boards. Mark mortises on inside faces of back legs and cut bare-faced tenons on lower back rail.

② Fitting Upper Back Rail to Back Leg
Mark mortise on ends of upper back rail (remember it is overlong) and cut out. Mark rail position on top of back legs and cut bare-faced tenons on legs. Cut excess from ends of rail to fit flush with back legs.

Mark up the ends of the slats for the two dowel holes (fig. 4) and, using a doweling jig, drill the ends of the slats to a depth of $\frac{7}{8}$in (22mm) using an $\frac{5}{16}$in (8mm) dowel (brad-point) drill bit.

Mark a center line along the top edge of the lower rail and the bottom edge of the upper rail for the center line of the dowel holes.

Work out the positions of the slats along one of these, adjusting as necessary to give an even spacing between the slats. Mark the centers of the dowel hole positions all the way along.

Clamp the two rails together and transfer the dowel center marks to the other rail. Drill the dowel holes to a depth of $\frac{7}{8}$in (22mm).

ASSEMBLING THE FRAME

Dry assemble the whole bench. Bevel the edges of the front and back legs, the lower side rails, the underside of the upper side rails, the edge of the lower back rail, and the underside of the front rail using either a router with a beveling bit or a power plane.

Sand all the components to smooth the faces and edges, and to clean off any pencil marks. Glue up the end frames using a gap-filling waterproof glue such as epoxy resin, clamping it tightly until the glue has thoroughly dried.

At this point, an adjustment has to be made to the height of the back legs to allow the seat to angle back slightly to assist rainwater drainage. This is done by standing the end frame on a flat surface, such as the workbench, and shimming the front edge of the front leg by $\frac{5}{8}$in (15mm) using a scrap piece of wood (fig. 5).

Using an offcut of the same thickness, scribe the back leg and the side and back of the front leg to the correct angle. Cut off the bottoms of the legs to these lines. Repeat for the other end frame. Glue the front rail and the lower back rail into the end frames, then glue all the dowels and slats into the lower back rail. Apply glue to the tops of the slats and to the dowels and seat-back tenons, then tap the upper back rail into place. You will need someone to help you with this.

THE SEAT

CONSTRUCTION

The seat is a solid piece formed by doweling together a number of narrow lengths of wood. Use a doweling jig and join to the frame with $\frac{5}{16}$in (8mm) dowels, $1\frac{1}{2}$in (40mm) long, spaced about 6–9in (150–225mm) apart.

After doweling, glue the lengths together using a gap-filling waterproof wood adhesive, such as epoxy resin, and hold the assembly together with bar clamps or folding wedges against a fixed board nailed to a worktop.

When the glue has dried, sand the surface flush and position the seat on the seat bench frame, leaving a $\frac{1}{8}$in (4mm) wide gap at the back for drainage. Mark around so that there is a $\frac{3}{4}$in (19mm) overhang at each end and at the front, then trim the seat to this line.

Cut a $\frac{1}{2}$in (12mm) chamfer on the top edges at the front and sides using either a router with a beading bit or a power plane.

INSTALLATION

Secure the seat in place using galvanized shrinkage plates – two at each end and three along the front – and screw into the seat rails and underside of the seat.

To keep the seat rigid so it will not bow in the middle, drill through the back rail into the seat in five places using a $\frac{1}{2}$in (12mm) spade bit. Drill about 2in (50mm) into the seat. Cut five lengths of $\frac{1}{2}$in (12mm) dowel about $3\frac{3}{4}$in (95mm) long. Use a tenon saw or the point of a nail to cut two grooves $\frac{1}{16}$–$\frac{1}{8}$in (2–4mm) deep along the dowel lengths to allow glue and air to escape as the dowels are driven into position.

Apply waterproof adhesive to the holes and hammer the dowels into position using the mallet. After the glue has set, saw off the protruding ends flush with the seat rail.

Bevel the bottom edges of the legs so the wood will not split if the bench is dragged on the ground. To prevent the legs from rotting, affix large, metal hammer-in glides to the bottoms of the legs.

❸ Shaping Upper Back Rail
Mark sides and back of back rail to follow taper of back face of back leg. Remove waste and plane smooth.

❹ Fitting the Back Slats
Mark slat and dowel positions on rails. Fit slats between back rails using two dowels each end.

❺ Angling the Legs
Above **Stand bench frame on a flat surface and shim front leg with scrap wood. Scribe legs as necessary.**

❻ Cross-section of Seat
Below **Seat boards are butted up and joined using dowels. Longer dowels affix seat to lower back rail.**

OCTAGONAL TREE SEAT

Even in the smallest garden, a tree seat makes an inviting point of interest. Any type of seating really makes a garden look furnished, but a seat which encircles a tree is particularly appealing. Children enjoy playing on, under, and around the shady platform and seem to gain endless amusement sitting on opposite sides from each other or their parents.

Although this seat looks complicated, it is actually fairly simple to make.

Nevertheless, it is a time-consuming project. Because the back leans inwards, cutting the back slats could have been quite a difficult proposition. To prevent unnecessary complication, a gap has been left between the slats to accommodate any discrepancies.

Other design simplifications were made. There is a simple bold structure for the frame underneath rather than mortise-and-tenon joints.

Softwood is an easy material to work with and contributes a great deal to the ease with which a structure like this can be made. But softwood does need to be protected in some way, by treating with preservative, and then by applying a final finish of wood stain or, as in this case, paint. Depending on where in your garden the seat is positioned, you might like to choose a brighter color: a strong blue would be very effective.

OCTAGONAL TREE SEAT

MATERIALS

Part	Quantity	Material	Length
BACK LEGS	8	2 × 3in (50 × 75mm) S4S softwood	42in (1050mm)
FRONT LEGS	8	As above	20in (500mm)
SEAT FRAME RAILS	32	1 × 3in (25 × 75mm) S4S softwood	21in (530mm)
SEAT SLATS	48	As above	As required
APRON BOARDS	8	As above	As required
BACK SLATS	72	$\frac{5}{8}$ × 2in (16 × 50mm) S4S softwood	As required
APRON BACK-UP BATTENS	8	1 × 1in (25 × 25mm) S4S softwood	6in (150mm) shorter than apron boards

Also required: waterproof woodworking adhesive; 1$\frac{1}{2}$in (38mm) No. 8 galvanized countersunk wood screws

The size of this eight-sided tree seat is governed by the size of the tree you wish to surround. Remember, you must leave room for the trunk to expand as the tree grows! Some trees grow faster than others: we built our seat around a small walnut tree, which is a slow-growing species, but even so we allowed an internal diameter of 24in (600mm) at the very top of the back support. Quite large tree specimens are available from good garden centers, so it could be worth planting a small

"standard" tree (that is, one with a long trunk) just as the focal point around which to build this seat.

The basic construction consists of eight separate frames on which the seat and backrest slats are affixed. The frames are of a predetermined size, but the length of the slats is varied according to the internal diameter of the seat.

The seat is made in two sections, dry assembled to each other, so the two halves can be easily unscrewed to install around the tree.

SEAT FRAMES

Cut the components of the seat frames to length.

Bevel the front face of each back leg at an angle of 22$\frac{1}{2}°$ from the center line of one of the 3in (75mm) faces (fig. 1). It is best to do this using a circular saw canted over at the correct angle – use a sliding bevel aligned on a protractor to set this. Finish off using a hand or power plane for a smooth finish.

1 **Beveling the Back Leg**
Draw a line down middle of front face of each back leg. Bevel legs at an angle of 22$\frac{1}{2}°$ from this line.

2 **Making the Spacing Template**
Cut a spacing template from a scrap piece of board to the dimensions shown below. The template is used for accurate positioning of the front and back legs and the seat frame rails to make up the seat frames.

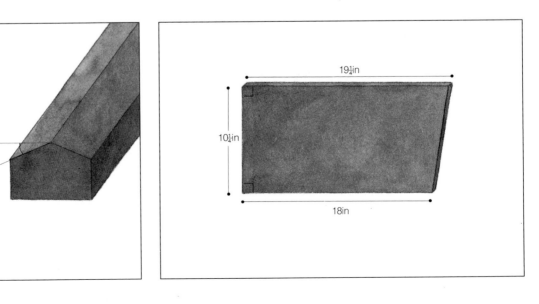

OCTAGONAL TREE SEAT ASSEMBLY

BACK LEG

BACK SLAT

SEAT FRAME

SEAT SLAT

APRON BOARD

SEAT FRAME RAIL

FRONT LEG

SEAT FRAME RAIL

OCTAGONAL TREE SEAT

Using a scrap of hardboard or plywood to the shape and dimensions shown (fig. 2, page 32), make up a template for attaching the seat frame rails to the front and back legs to make up the seat frames.

Temporarily nail a batten to your workbench to give a flat surface to rest the feet of the legs against. Lay the front and back legs of one frame on the bench with two seat frame rails on top and the spacing template between them (fig. 1). The back leg must be angled to align with the back of the template and the front leg should be exactly flush with the front edge of the template. The bottom of the legs should be resting against the batten nailed to the workbench.

The bottom seat frame rail is positioned so that it overlaps the front leg by ½in (12mm), while the top frame rail should be flush with the front and top of the front leg.

If a suitable flat workbench is not

DETAIL OF SEAT LEGS

Gravel-filled holes around the front and back legs of the seat frames make leveling easier and keep the legs off water-logged ground, reducing the risk of the wood rotting.

② Finished Construction of the Seat Frames
Above Glue and screw seat frame rails to legs, then trim overlap at the back so it is parallel with slope of back leg and protrudes ½in (12mm). *Below* Finished frame shows frame rails screwed in position to front and back legs.

① Making Up the Seat Frames
Lay the front and back legs of one frame on a flat surface so they are flush with template. Top frame rail rests on template and is flush with the top and front of front rail; bottom frame rail overlaps front leg by ½in (12mm).

½in

available for this setting out, the pieces can be laid out on a flat floor, with the legs resting against an adjacent wall, so that the wall aligns the base of the legs.

Glue the top of the seat frame rail in place using a waterproof woodworking adhesive (ideally an epoxy resin), then drill pilot holes and screw it to the front and back legs using two screws at each end. Glue and screw the bottom seat frame rail to the legs in the same way.

Turn the frame over and position the other two seat frame rails in the same way, top and bottom. It is very important that these rails are exactly square to the ones on the other side so that the rails will be flush across the top where the seat slats will be fixed (fig. 2).

To complete the construction of the frames, the seat frame rails are trimmed off in line with the back leg, but leaving a $\frac{1}{2}$in (12mm) overlap (fig. 2). Strike a line at this position, and then trim off using a small crosscut saw or circular saw.

Repeat the construction for the remaining seven frames.

SEAT SLATS

The seat slats are cut from 1 × 3in (25 × 75mm) S4S (smooth 4 sides) softwood. The dimensions of the seat frames are predetermined, so that the number of slats required will not vary, no matter how large the finished seat. What you will have to calculate yourself, however, is the length of each slat. This will depend upon the internal diameter of the seat, itself dependent on size of the tree trunk around which you assemble the project.

To measure for the seat section, stand the eight frames around the tree roughly in position and spaced at the required distance from the tree, allowing for growth and depending on how large you want the diameter of the tree seat.

MAKING THE SEAT SLATS

When you are satisfied with the spacing of the seat frames, measure the distance between the centers of the back legs at seat height and calculate the average ("x" in fig. 3).

This will be the length of the inside edge of the innermost seat slats (ours are 15in [380mm] long).

Mark length "x" onto the back edge of a piece of the slat wood and draw 112$\frac{1}{2}$° angles off at either end using a sliding bevel. You can then use this slat to help draw up a full-size plan of a seat section (fig. 4) which will enable you to cut the remaining five seat slats to the correct length.

To make the full-size plan, mark off the back measurement using the innermost slat as a guide for the angles. Extend the angled lines outwards, using the sliding bevel to double check that the angle is 112$\frac{1}{2}$°. Returning to the seat frame, measure the distance from the center of the back leg to the front of the frame ("y" in fig. 3). On a full-size plan, mark the length "y" on the angled lines, and add $\frac{3}{4}$in (20mm) to allow for the approximate thickness of the apron board at the front of the seat. Join up the two marks "y plus $\frac{3}{4}$in (20mm)" at the front of the plan, parallel with the back line, to give the front edge of the seat.

You can now work out the necessary spacing for the slats. Place the innermost slat in position on the full-size plan and roughly cut five more slats, making sure that they are overlong. Bunch the slats together against the innermost slat, measure the remaining distance to the front line of the seat, and divide by five to give the amount of space to be left between each slat. If you want to increase the spacing, at this stage plane the edge of the innermost slat to reduce its width.

Using one of the slats and a spacing batten or spacing blocks cut to the width of the calculated space, draw out all six slats in position on the full-size plan. You will then be able to measure off the plan for the exact lengths of all the slats in each section of the seat.

Cut out all the slats for one seat section, but cut about $\frac{1}{16}$in (2mm) inside each marked line in order to create a deliberate gap between the ends of the slats. You can use the slats cut for the first seat frame as templates for cutting the seat slats for the other sections.

③ Measuring up for the Seat Slats
Measure distance between centers of back legs at seat height ("x") to calculate length of innermost slat. Measure distance between center of back leg and front of frame ("y") to calculate spacing between slats.

④ Drawing up Full-size Plan of Seat Section
Mark length "x" and draw lines "y plus $\frac{3}{4}$in (20mm)" either end at 112$\frac{1}{2}$° angle. Bunch six slats on plan, measure remaining distance to front and divide by five to calculate spacing. Cut spacers to size, then mark slat positions.

OCTAGONAL TREE SEAT

AFFIXING THE SEAT SLATS

Affix the innermost slats first. Place the first slat across the back of two seat frames, spaced about $\frac{1}{16}$in (2mm) in from the center of the back legs, then glue and screw the slat to the top seat frame rails with one screw at each end (fig. 1).

Take another seat frame and innermost slat, and space in the same way. Glue and screw in place as before.

Continue in this way for two groups of three sections each. It is very important that you only dry assemble two sections opposite one another, as you will need to remove the slats on two opposite sides of the structure in order to install the seat frames around the tree.

To affix the subsequent slats, line up the next shortest slat with the innermost slat (fig. 2). With the spacing batten (or blocks) between the slats, align one end of the new slat with a batten held against one end of the previously affixed slat. Glue and screw into the top seat frame rail at each end.

Continue with this second size slat all the way around, remembering only to dry assemble where you did before. Continue in this fashion, one row at a time, assembling without glue those slats in the two sections that are dry assembled.

Before the frontmost slats are fitted, the apron boards must be assembled (fig. 3). Cut a piece of 1 × 3in (25 × 75mm) wood to the longest length of the frontmost slat and bevel back the edges at each end so they are in line with the angles of the seat slat. Cut a 1 × 1in (25 × 25mm) back-up batten about 6in (150mm) shorter than the apron board and glue and screw it centrally in place to join the apron board to the frontmost slat. The front edge of the slat must be flush with the front face of the apron board. Repeat the process to make the other apron boards.

Round off the front edges of the frontmost slats to give a smooth finish. Glue and screw into place at the front edges of the frames, remembering not to glue the dry assembled sections.

THE BACK SLATS

The back of each seat section is comprised of nine slats, cut from $\frac{5}{8}$ × 2in (16 × 50mm) S4S (smooth 4 sides) softwood. However, because the back legs of the frame are angled, the slats are not all the same length; instead, they get shorter as they reach the top.

Decide on the spacing of the back slats, and use scrap pieces of wood of the required thickness as spacing blocks. Lay the spacing blocks at seat level so that you start with a space, then lay the first slat, left overlong for the time being, in position. Mark off the ends in line with the centers of the back legs (fig. 4). Set a sliding bevel to this angle, and cut the back slat to the marked length. Use the sliding bevel to mark off the correct angle and cut the first slats for the remaining back sections to length. Glue and screw the first back slats in place to the front of the back legs of all the seat sections, but leave the slats dry assembled in the same sections as you did before on the seat slats.

Use the spacing blocks to position the next length of slat (fig. 4), mark off the ends as before, and cut to length. Repeat for the other seven slats in the row around the seat, and affix as before.

Continue in this way, row by row, until the seat back is completed (nine rows in our case). If the back legs protrude above the top slats they can be cut flush with the top of the slats for a neat appearance.

Dismantle the dry joints so that the seat is in two "halves" (actually, two three-eighths).

ASSEMBLY

Take the two "halves" of the seat to the tree and partially reassemble it without glue so you can mark on the ground where the legs are positioned. Dismantle the seat again.

At the leg positions, dig holes for each of the 16 legs, 6in (150mm) in diameter and 6in (150mm) deep, and fill them with gravel. The gravel provides good drainage, reducing the risk of the legs rotting, and allows you to level the seat easily.

1 Affixing the Innermost Seat Slats
Use plan as guide but cut slats about $\frac{1}{16}$in (2mm) short both ends. Space slat about $\frac{1}{16}$in (2mm) in from center of back legs; affix between two top frame rails. Work around frames, but *dry assemble* slats on two facing sections.

2 Affixing Subsequent Slats to the Frame
Align next shortest slat with innermost slat: put the spacers or spacing battens in position, align ends of slat with innermost slat, and affix to frame rails. Continue around frame, then repeat for next size slats.

FINISHING

Before painting, it is important to treat the seat with a good-quality wood preservative which can be painted over when dry – most clear sealers available fall into this category. We applied two coats, allowing each to dry thoroughly, and stood the legs in dishes of preservative for a couple of days.

Once the wood preservative is thoroughly dry (allow at least a week), the seat can be painted. We used a microporous paint which needs no primer (apart from preservative) and is intended for outdoor use. The seat can be treated with a water-repellent preservative stain if a natural finish is preferred.

After finishing with paint or wood stain, the seat can be finally assembled around the tree. Make sure the seat is well-bedded in the gravel and stands level on the ground. You can glue all joints at final assembly, or leave two sections of slats "dry" to allow easy removal of the seat should the need arise.

❸ Making the Apron Board

Above Use batten to attach apron board to frontmost slat. *Below* Front edge rounded over.

❹ Spacing and Affixing the Back Slats

Back slats are initially overlong. Use spacing batten or spacing blocks to position back slat, and mark off ends of slat to line up with centers of back legs. Cut slats to length, then reposition and glue and screw in place.

BARBECUE

Most barbecues, whether they are home-made or ready-made versions, have a number of design problems. One common fault is that they are generally too low to work at comfortably, which means the cook spends most of the time crouched awkwardly over the grill. The second problem is that grilling areas are often too small, providing food for only a limited number of people at a time.

This barbecue area corrects both of these typical defects, as well as providing a carefully considered series of spaces and surfaces for serving the food, storing fuel, and keeping pans and dishes.

The generous grill area can be temporarily reduced in size if you only want to cook a small amount of food by placing bricks in the middle and confining the space in that way. The grill supports consist of several strips of angle iron cemented into place and these hold the grill tray. The entire structure is built up against a brick wall. With time, the wall will blacken with smoke, but this is not an unattractive effect. If you do not have a similar site for the barbecue, you can build a small brick wall at the back instead or leave the barbecue free-standing.

One particular advantage of this construction is the spaces it provides at either end of the grill area as well as beneath. On top, two quite extensive surfaces can be used as a place for resting pans and dishes of food in preparation. Underneath, wood can be stored. If you use the barbecue often and for long enough, the whole structure will warm up and the timber will be "kiln-dried."

BARBECUE

Few pleasures are equal to that of sitting outside on a warm, summer's evening, eating food in the company of family and friends. If you build a barbecue, it will add a second focal point to your sitting-out area, but be careful to site it away from overhanging plants and any other vegetation that might catch fire while you are cooking.

The barbecue here is built from reclaimed bricks which match the wall against which it is built. Second-hand bricks are marginally larger than new bricks, but the dimensions here are calculated in courses rather than specific measurements, and you can use either sort of brick for building this project. The grill area is large enough to cook a substantial amount of food, but you could build the ends closer together if preferred.

The barbecue can be built against an existing wall or it can be free-standing. You can either build it on top of concrete pavers, or you can lay the pavers around the barbecue once it has been built. If you choose the latter option, you will have to cut the pavers to fit, and you will also need to construct a foundation before laying the first course of bricks. The foundation will need to be at least 6in (150mm) deep and 8in (200mm) wide around the outline of the barbecue. Lay 4in (100mm) of gravel in the trench, ram it down, and then cover it with a 2in (50mm) layer of concrete. Check that the surface is level, and then leave the base to dry out and harden for a day or so.

As long as the pavers are level and are correctly laid on a firm base, however, it will be easier to build the barbecue on existing pavers. It is a good idea to protect the paving on which the barbecue is to be built with a sheet of thick, heavy-duty polyethylene. Simply lay the polyethylene sheet over the pavers, build up the barbecue on top of the polyethylene, and then cut away the protruding sheet afterwards. The polyethylene will protect the surface of the paving from staining with wet cement while you are building, and will keep the brickwork at the base clean and dry.

CONSTRUCTION

Lay the bricks following the course-by-course plans (figs. 1–3; *see also* **Techniques: Bricklaying, pages 156–7**). You will find it helpful to lay out this project to ensure that the side walls are built exactly at right angles to the rear wall. A builder's square is quite easy to make from three battens with lengths in the proportion of 3:4:5. These should be nailed together to form a right-angled triangle – a useful size of square to make is a triangle with a base measuring 18in (450mm), a height of 24in (600mm) and a hypotenuse of 30in (750mm). Leave all of the battens slightly overlong, then nail or screw them together to form *exactly* these dimensions. Saw off the surplus afterward.

Using a tight string line and the builder's square, make sure that the bricks in each course are straight and, using a carpenter's level, make sure that each course is vertical.

When the seventh course is reached, set angle irons across the central section to support bricks forming the firebed. Do *not* lay these bricks for the time being.

Lay the eighth to eleventh courses, and on the eleventh course bed mild steel strips across the side walls to support the "table" tops.

Spread the mortar on the strips, then lay the twelfth course. Finally, lay bedding mortar on the angle irons in the central section and lay the firebed bricks edge on.

After the mortar has dried out, drill the bricks in the eleventh and twelfth courses to take steel supports (lag screws with the heads cut off are ideal) which will hold the food grill tray above the firebed. Measure the size of the central opening and get a local steel fabricator to make a grill tray by welding an outer frame of mild steel strips, braced with mild steel strips and fitted with mild steel rods welded at intervals about 1in (25mm) apart.

To protect the bricks of the firebed from excessive heat and to keep them clean, at the same time that the grill is made, a steel tray can be made up to cover the firebed.

TOOLS

BRICKLAYER'S TROWEL

POINTING TROWEL

BRICKLAYER'S HAMMER

BRICKLAYER'S CHISEL

SHOVEL

BUCKET

BUILDER'S SQUARE

CARPENTER'S LEVEL (long)

MATERIALS

BRICKS – 231 new or second-hand

MORTAR – from cement and builder's sand in the proportion 1:6

STEEL ANGLE IRONS – 4 pieces, 40in (1016mm) long

MILD STEEL STRIPS – 6 pieces, 4 × 12in (100 × 300mm)

MILD STEEL – for grill; measure finished barbecue for exact dimensions

1 *Above* **Plan View of 1st, 3rd, 5th and 7th Courses**
Lay bricks as shown; bed angle irons to support firebed on 7th course only.
Below **Plan view of 2nd, 4th and 6th Courses**
Cut three-quarter length bricks to enable courses to be staggered.

BARBECUE ASSEMBLY

FOOD GRILL TRAY

$2\frac{1}{2}$ BRICKS

12 BRICKS

12 BRICKS ON EDGE

FIREBED

STEEL REINFORCEMENT STRIPS

ANGLE IRON

2 *Above* **Plan View of 8th Course**
Two rows of 12 bricks are laid edge on above angle irons to form firebed
Below **Plan View of 9th and 11th Courses**
From 9th course, bricks only laid at ends; steel plates above 11th course.

3 *Above* **Plan View of 10th Course**
Lay six bricks each end as shown.
Below **Plan View of 12th Course**
Ten bricks each end are laid above steel strips to form top.

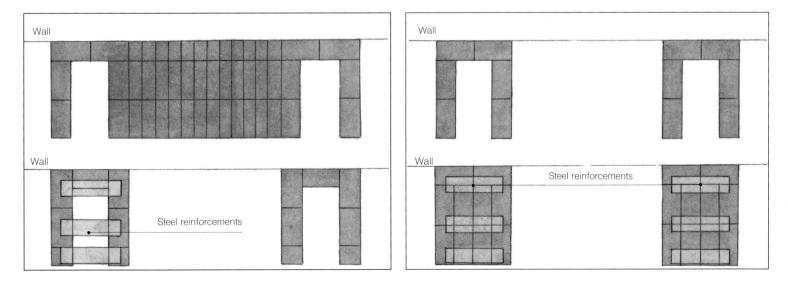

Wall

Wall

Steel reinforcements

Wall

Wall

Steel reinforcements

AWNING

An awning over a patio or terrace area gives privacy and allows you to use the area in most weather. The awning here is an optional addition to a simple pergola attached to a house wall. It rests on the pergola and can be brought out in sunny or warm showery weather, yet is simple to remove when not required.

You can make the pergola more or less any size to suit your patio or paved area. The structure is made from planed stock; western red cedar is ideal, but ordinary preservative treated softwood coated with a water-repellent wood stain is a very serviceable alternative.

The supporting posts are made from 4 × 4in (100 × 100mm) lumber of sufficient length to give headroom of at least 7ft 6in (2.3m) under the pergola structure. The posts are positioned about 8ft (2.4m) apart and are linked to the house wall by 2 × 8in (50 × 200mm) roof joists. At the front, the posts are steadied and separated at the top by a fascia board measuring 1½ × 4in (38 × 100mm) which runs the entire length of the pergola.

In the example shown, where there is a wall at the end of the terrace, there is no need to position a post and roof joist against the house wall. Instead, a length of 2 × 4in (50 × 100mm) lumber is bolted to the wall so that the top of this length of lumber is at the same level as the tops of the roof joists. Use expansion bolts to ensure a secure attachment.

On the main wall of the house, the roof joists can be supported in galvanized steel joist hangers, which are screwed and anchored to the house wall; the roof joists are then screwed into the joist hangers. An alternative method for supporting the roof joists is to rest them on a 2 × 4in (50 × 100mm) wooden beam (called a wall plate) which is fixed horizontally to the wall, using expansion bolts, so that it supports the roof joists at the correct height. In this case, the roof joists can be affixed to the wall plate by nailing at an angle through the sides of the roof joists and into the top of the wall plate (see **Techniques, Toe-nailing, page 151**).

An unusual but practical feature of this pergola is the covered roof section close to the wall of the house. This provides permanent shelter and shade at the back of the seating area, and also strengthens the pergola, prevents sideways movement in high winds, and keeps rain off the house window frames.

The removable awning is made from deck chair canvas and is intended to be fitted during the warmer months of the year. It is draped across the roof joists and is held in place by tapes that loop around the roof joists. The tapes are secured by Velcro fasteners. The awning is stiffened at each end by being folded over and tacked to a ⅜ × ¾in (9.5 × 19mm) strip of hardwood such as yellow birch.

CONSTRUCTION

Start by cutting the support posts to length. You need to take into account that the roof joists are affixed at a slight downward slope, and that you might not have a great deal of flexibility over the height at which you can affix the joist hangers or wall plate to the wall of your house. You also need to decide how the posts will be secured at the bottom. The easiest method is to slot them into socket-type supports which can be screwed to the surface of the patio (fig. 2). Alternatively, each post can be fitted over a protruding bolt or bracket cemented into the surface of the paving. Yet another option is to chip a hole through the surface of the patio using a hammer and cold chisel so that the bottom of the post can be concreted in place.

Once the length of post has been decided, the top can be angled and the joint cut to accommodate the roof joist. Saw down to form a slot to suit the width of the roof joist – its actual width will be less than 2in (50mm). Most of the waste can be removed by sawing, and the joint (a form of mortise and tenon joint) can be cleaned up using a chisel.

If the roof joists will be affixed to the house wall using joist hangers, these are installed next. Make sure that they are level by lining them up with a line drawn along the wall.

1 Detail of Top Section

The roof joists are supported by 4 × 4in (100 × 100mm) posts at the front and by the main wall of the house at the back. Shade is provided by the permanent covered section and the removable canvas awning.

2 Socket-type Post Supports

Metal support is screwed or bolted to ground. Post slots in support and is secured by tightening screws.

Check that the line is horizontal using a carpenter's level and affix the joist hangers using galvanized screws into anchors. Alternatively, affix the wall plate in place using expansion bolts. Slot the roof joists in place between the post and joist hanger or wall plate, and secure with a bolt through the post, and by screwing through the joist hanger. Toe nail the joists if they are resting on a wall plate (fig. 3). Nail the fascia board to the top of the support posts.

All that remains is to install the permanent covered section (fig. 4). Nail $\frac{1}{2} \times 1\frac{1}{2}$in (12 × 38mm) cedar or stained softwood slats across the joists finishing with a 1 × 1$\frac{1}{2}$in (25 × 38mm) batten which is notched at intervals to accept the roof joists and is fitted vertically against the lowest slat. The top is covered with a 36in- (915mm-) deep sheet of $\frac{3}{4}$in exterior grade plywood which is then covered with roofing felt or shingles. The roof-to-wall joint is sealed by pressing a strip of self-adhesive flashing across the entire length of the joint.

③ Affixing the Joists to the Wall
Left Joist hangers are aligned at correct height and screwed to wall; joists sit in hangers and are screwed in place. *Right* 2 × 4in (50 × 100mm) wall plate secured horizontally to wall; joists toe nailed in place.

④ Permanent Covered Section
Softwood slats are nailed to roof joists. Batten at front of slats is notched at intervals to accept joists. Section is then covered in exterior-grade plywood and building paper and shingles. Seal roof-to-wall joint with flashing strip.

Joist hanger

Roof joist

Roof joist

Wall plate

Flashing strip

Building paper and shingles

Plywood

Slats

Notched batten

Roof joist

WOODEN TABLE

This sturdy garden table makes an attractive feature in any outdoor setting. The table shown is only 15in (375mm) high, but by increasing the height of the base on which it is built you can make it to any height required. If you make it about 30in (750mm) high, for example, you will be able to sit around it on garden chairs and use it as an outdoor dining table.

Apart from the brick base, the table is made entirely from solid wood. Preservative-treated quality softwood is ideal; hardwood could be used, but because of the large quantity of lumber required, its cost would be prohibitively high.

The table top is made from 2×3in (50×75mm) lumber, in the form of 12 square frames which become progressively larger from a central block. There is a gap of about $\frac{1}{2}$in (12mm) between each square, which is created by using 2in (50mm) wide S4S (smooth 4 sides) lumber for the table top. S4S lumber is sawn to its nominal width – in this case 2in (50mm) – and then each face is planed about $\frac{1}{2}$in (12mm) so that the actual width is about $1\frac{1}{2}$in (38mm).

CONSTRUCTION

Start by building a base from brick, stone or reconstituted stone-and-concrete blocks (see **Techniques, page 157**); the base should measure 22×22in (560×560mm) and it should be about 9in (225mm) high if you want to make the table as shown in the photograph. The height could be increased to as much as 24in (600mm) if an outdoor dining table is required.

The table top is fixed on two diagonal supports which are fitted to the base plinth to form an "X." Cut cross lap joints (see **Techniques, page 152**) at the point where the supports intersect (fig. 2). For neatness, the ends of the supports are sloped as shown in the side view

(fig. 2). The last 12in (300mm) is sloped from the nominal depth of 3in (75mm) to 1in (25mm) at the end. Assemble the supports by gluing the cross lap joint with waterproof woodworking adhesive and then clamp the supports until the glue sets, checking first that the supports are exactly at right angles.

If you are unable to buy preservative pressure-treated lumber, then at this stage it is wise to treat the supports with a good quality water-repellent preservative; apply a second coat of preservative 24 hours later.

The supports are fixed down to the base plinth using expansion bolts into holes drilled in the base plinth and recessed into the supports. Before tightening these bolts, check that the supports are absolutely level using a carpenter's level and put shim pieces underneath them to adjust as necessary.

FORMING THE TABLE TOP

The table top consists of concentric "frames" which fit one inside the other down to the solid block

MATERIALS

Part	Quantity	Material	Length
PLINTH	As required	Bricks or concrete blocks	As required
TABLE-TOP SUPPORTS	2	2×3in (50×75mm) S4S softwood	67in (1700mm)
TABLE-TOP FRAMES	4	2×3in (50×75mm) S4S softwood	48in (1200mm)
	4	As above	44in (1100mm)
	4	As above	40in (1000mm)
	4	As above	36in (900mm)
	4	As above	32in (800mm)
	4	As above	28in (700mm)
	4	As above	24in (600mm)
	4	As above	20in (500mm)
	4	As above	16in (400mm)
	4	As above	12in (300mm)
	4	As above	8in (200mm)
	4	As above	4in (100mm)

ALSO: about 48ft (15m) of $\frac{3}{8}$in (9.5mm) diameter hardwood dowel to be cut into 4in (100mm) lengths for joining corners; 4 expansion bolts for securing table-top supports; waterproof woodworking adhesive.

① Brick Plinth Base
Table rests on brick or stone plinth built to required height. Fill middle with rubble topped with concrete.

② Making the Table-top Supports
Cut cross lap joints in the supports so that they meet to form an "X," with the supports exactly at right angles. The ends of the supports are sloped on the underside through the last 12in (300mm).

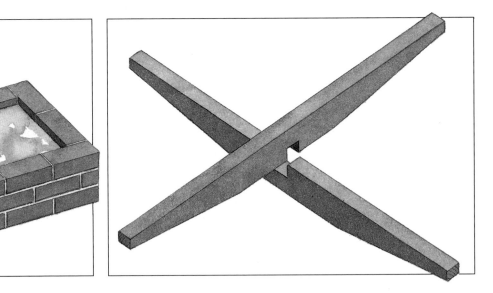

formed of four pieces in the center. Although the stock is 2 × 3in (50 × 75mm), the "frames" are formed just like giant picture frames, with the corners mitered at 45°. The easiest way to cut these miters is to use a power saw with the blade tilted to a 45° angle. You can use an ordinary portable circular power saw with the lumber held securely in a vise, but it will be even easier to make the cuts if you hire or buy a miter saw, a radial arm saw, or a circular saw table for the purpose.

Cut the largest frame so that it gives external dimensions of 48 × 48in (1200 × 1200mm). Apply waterproof woodworking adhesive to the mating parts of each joint, then draw them together with frame clamps before drilling into the joint with a ⅜in (9.5mm) drill bit, keeping the bit at a 90° angle to the joint. Drill two holes in each joint and then drive ⅜in (9.5mm) long wooden dowels into the holes, after coating the dowels with waterproof woodworking adhesive. Before applying the adhesive, make a shallow saw cut along the length of each dowel, which will help to ensure that not all of the glue will be driven out when the dowel is inserted. At this stage, make sure that the dowel is long enough to protrude from the hole at each end; when the adhesive has set, the ends of the dowels can be sawn off close to the sides of the frame and the surface then neatly planed smooth to give an unobtrusive fixture. Make up the remaining frames in the same way to the dimensions specified in the Materials chart (opposite).

The central block is formed by cutting four pieces of 2 × 3in (50 × 75mm) lumber sections which are joined by dowels to form a square block. The frames are treated with two coats of water-repellent wood preservative before being assembled on to the wooden supports.

The table-top frames are attached to the table-top supports using waterproof woodworking adhesive and dowels inserted into holes drilled vertically down into the supports and vertically up into the undersides of the table-top frames.

❸ Affixing Table-top Supports to Plinth
Use expansion bolts to affix the supports at each corner of the plinth. Drill the plinth to accept the bolts and drill 2in (50mm) deep holes to recess the bolts in the supports. Check supports are level before final attachment.

❹ Forming Table-top Frames
Cut 45° miters at corners and affix using waterproof adhesive and dowels through the sides.

❺ Affixing Frames to Supports
Drill corresponding holes down into supports and up into corners of frames. Join using dowel joints.

PART 2

GARDEN HOUSES

The garden house is a subject in itself. At one extreme, garden houses can be supremely romantic, providing a true retreat from the world; at the other, they can be as mundane as a shed. In between come summer garden houses, gazebos, pavilions, follies, greenhouses, workshops, playhouses, studios, offices, and garden rooms. One could even include dovecotes, pigeon lofts, rabbit hutches, dog kennels, and chicken coops, since animal houses so often accompany human ones. But whatever their ultimate function, there is something uniquely appealing about buildings on such a small scale. For the garden designer, they are places where wit and imagination, as much as practicality, can come into play.

Children have inspired some of the most charming versions of the garden house, while animal houses, when they are decorated rather than strictly functional, also tend to be designed to amuse and appeal to children. More than any other type of garden structure, the many varieties of garden house offer the opportunity to use bright paints, providing a much-needed splash of year-round color to the garden.

GARDEN HOUSES

The summer house or garden retreat has a long tradition in Europe and an even longer tradition in the Far East. As a pavilion or gazebo it was essentially built to provide a platform from which to view a garden or, in Eastern terms, to contemplate nature. However, from the eighteenth century onward, the nature of the garden house evolved from being a viewing place to a kind of architectural attraction in the garden. Chinese pavilions, Japanese tea houses, miniature thatched cottages, classical temples, and Gothic grottoes were some of the styles that were enthusiastically embraced.

As a rule, follies of this kind really need acres of parkland to act as a foil for their charms; today, however, garden houses are usually simpler in design, reflecting their essentially practical nature. Nevertheless there are many attractive "ordinary" buildings to act as inspiration, including bathing huts, lodges, and gypsy caravans. Painted wood, clapboarding, shingle, and exterior-grade plywood are all good basic construction materials. Roofs can be tiled, shingled, or made of corrugated metal; for a truly rustic look, you could seek out a thatcher, or have the roof covered in turf. Building a garden house can be an exercise in creative salvage and recycling for those with that kind of imagination and skill.

The degree of finish depends on the ultimate use of the house: a building which must function as an annex for overnight guests obviously needs to be completed to a higher standard of comfort than one which merely serves as a place to read a book or escape from the rain. If you are going to use the house as a studio or office, for example, you will need to put in electricity; in other cases, having a supply of water might be a distinct advantage. Similarly, building permission may have to be sought from your local government department, depending on the intended size, function, and location of your structure.

Site is an important issue. A summer garden house or pavilion plays an obvious role in the layout of the entire garden. If you are going to sit there and admire nature, the view must be worthwhile.

HOME AWAY FROM HOME

The garden house – shed, pavilion, workshop, or summer garden house – is innately appealing (left and far left). Part of the charm of these small-scale buildings is their forthright style and use of simple materials.

Ample garden storage is an invaluable asset (above). Wall-mounted racks are generally a good idea; hanging tools saves floor space and prevents tines and blades becoming damaged. Ceiling hooks can be used to suspend baskets.

GARDEN HOUSES

Paving and planting should be planned taking into account the site of the building as far as possible. You could arrange for a pavilion to be set at the end of a walkway to give impact to a formal design, placed on a higher level to offer a view, or secreted in a sheltered corner to add a sense of mystery and surprise.

Although there is nothing mysterious or romantic about a garden shed, with a little thought it need not be the unlovely and somewhat blatant feature common to so many gardens. A garden shed which functions as a true garden room for maintenance of tools, potting, and storing seeds and bulbs is an invaluable resource in any household.

Storage is one of the main requirements. You will fill a shed very quickly with outdoor and garden equipment, so it is important to build or buy one which is big enough for your needs. The first consideration is likely to be providing an efficient system for storing garden tools, seeds, bulbs, fertilizer, and so on.

In addition to tool storage, you will need floor space for big items, which may include a lawnmower, bicycles, garden furniture, awnings and umbrellas packed away during the winter, portable barbecues, and large toys. You will also need somewhere to put bags of compost and charcoal, as well as a dry, high shelf for storing fertilizers and pesticides out of the reach of children and animals. Ceiling hooks can be used to accommodate baskets and buckets; shelves will take pots and seed trays. It is also useful to have somewhere cool and dark for storing bulbs or root vegetables during the summer or after the harvest.

One advantage of a well-planned storage system is that you can see at a glance if anything has not been put back. But the benefits are not merely practical. As well as providing an efficient area to work, a carefully organized garden room or shed, with its array of traditional garden tools and equipment, can be as pleasant a place in which to spend time as a kitchen.

As far as site is concerned, there is no reason why a shed needs to be in full view. You may not have all that much choice when it comes to position, but it is a good idea to place the shed out of the way, near a compost heap or bonfire site. Alternatively, you can create a utility area by positioning the shed near an existing garage or greenhouse and screen the view by adding trellis panels or fencing and climbing plants.

Off-the-shelf sheds, which come in ready-to-assemble packs, are rarely as attractive as those you design and build yourself. But there are ways of improving the appearance of the standard shed which are especially useful if you have little choice about where the shed is positioned. Many examples look better if they are simply painted. Good quality brick pavers laid around the base, plant tubs filled with flowers, and trellis with plants trained over will all help to connect the shed to its surroundings, making it look less brash and out of place.

GARDEN RETREATS

A garden house can provide a secluded spot for sitting and watching the world go by (far left, center and far right). If you want to disguise a structure or hide an ugly shed from view, fast-growing climbers are the answer.

ANIMAL HOUSES

Coops, dovecotes, birdhouses, and the like can be the excuse for wit and decorative flair to come into play. These structures provide a good opportunity to practice remodeling skills.

SUMMER GARDEN HOUSE

Most people could use the extra space that a summer garden house provides. And although this is the perfect place for storing tools, bulbs and seeds, or for potting plants or a variety of other garden chores, you need not necessarily put it to horticultural use. A workshop, an artist's studio, a guest annex, the ultimate playhouse – it is easy to think of a host of functions for this kind of structure to fulfil. It could prove invaluable as a home office or study, and it is substantial enough to serve as a pavilion on a village green. However, the use it is put to can mean that you will have to seek approvals and permits from local authorities. It is best to check during the planning stages, well before you start building.

The house may appear a daunting prospect for all but the most ardent enthusiast; but the skills you require are well within the average range of ability and there is no need for the kind of refinement demanded by furniture-making. There is no sophisticated joinery and there are few techniques which should not already be familiar. The cost of materials, all readily available, is roughly the same as a family vacation, which makes it fairly reasonable, unless you put a high price on your own time and labor. The major commitment is time. Working alone during the evenings and weekends, it should take about three months. Full-time, with a few willing assistants, it might take only a couple of weeks.

As far as the design is concerned, there were a number of influences. The idea to use corrugated metal for the roof came from the houses of the Australian outback. The shape of the roof was suggested by the roofline of the traditional English cricket pavilion. In different color combinations, the house acquires quite different aspects: green and white for a cricket pavilion; pale pastels for a seaside look; bright blues and pinks for the Caribbean.

The project is a major undertaking. We would recommend that you attempt most of the other projects in the book before tackling this one. But if the demands are high, so are the rewards. What could be more satisfying – or useful – than building your own garden house?

SUMMER GARDEN HOUSE

A summer garden house, somewhere in a secluded part of the yard, is a delightful retreat to be savored when you want to relax away from the bustle of the house. This design captures all the magic, charm and intrigue required from a garden hideaway and just invites you to explore inside. The size of the room is about 8 × 12ft (2.4 × 3.6m) which is a comfortable size to furnish with wicker chairs yet remains cozy and intimate. The extended roof covering over the veranda gives the impression of greater size while providing a 39in (1000mm) deep protected area on showery days when you want to sit outside. The size of the base is critical in determining whether you need building permission; location within your yard and the use for which the building is intended are also important. Check codes with your local authority during the planning stage.

The red-and-blue color scheme chosen here not only accentuates the design and materials but is fun, too. By changing the color combinations you can substantially alter the finished look of the building; a few suggestions for alternative colors are illustrated on page 67.

The basic structure rests on a level base of concrete pavers which in turn supports the joists. The veranda is pressure treated wooden boards, while the interior floor is exterior-grade plywood finished, in this case, with floor paint, although you could equally well use carpets, tiles, or boards. It is possible to extend the walls to include the veranda area if you require more indoor floor space. The interior walls are also clad with plywood to give the structure rigidity – between this and the exterior boarding is a layer of insulation. The level ceiling is covered in tongue-and-groove

boards and is also insulated. You could leave the roof structure exposed if you wanted, although you would lose a lot of heat in cold weather as a result. If you require heating, a paraffin heater or a fan heater are the best options.

The chains leading down from the gutter at the four corners of the building act in the same way as the drainpipes, conducting water down to the ground, where four drywells are dug: a feature of traditional Japanese houses.

The illustrations below and opposite give an overall impression of the construction of the front, back, and side walls and of the roof. However, in addition to the project text and illustrations, you may also need to refer to the sections on Materials and Techniques (pages 146–7 and 148–57) when further guidance is needed on individual stages of the construction.

TOOLS

PORTABLE WORKBENCH

STEEL MEASURING TAPE

STEEL BENCH RULE

TRY SQUARE or COMBINATION SQUARE

ADJUSTABLE T-BEVEL

SMALL CROSSCUT SAW (or circular saw)

POWER DRILL

DRILL BIT – $\frac{1}{2}$in (12mm) and $\frac{1}{8}$in (3.2mm)

WRENCH

HAMMER

NAILSET

PLIERS

CHISEL

MALLET

TIN SNIPS

CAPPING PIECE

CORRUGATED SHEET

FLASHING

GUTTER

FASCIA BOARD

POST

EXTERIOR CLADDING

TONGUED-AND-GROOVED BOARDS

JOIST

EXTERIOR CLADDING

ROOF CAPPING

FLASHING

EXTERIOR CLADDING

POST

PAVERS

CEILING JOIST

MAIN ROOF TRUSS

INTERMEDIATE PURLIN

RIDGE PURLIN

RAISED ROOF PURLIN

JACK RAFTER HEAD PLATE

END JACK RAFTER

GUTTER

SHORT CEILING RAFTER

BLOCKING

INSULATION

POST

PLYWOOD FLOOR

JOIST

SUMMER GARDEN HOUSE: BASE ASSEMBLY

FACING BOARD

POST

PLYWOOD FLOOR

TRIMMER

JOIST

PAVER (24 × 24 × 1½in)

HALF PAVER (24 × 12 × 1½in)

BASE ASSEMBLY

1 **Setting Out Position of Base**
Use pegs and stringline to set out base outline. Two sizes of paver are used – 24 × 24in (600 × 600mm) and 24 × 12in (600 × 300mm) – to support joists centrally while leaving a narrow border around house perimeter.

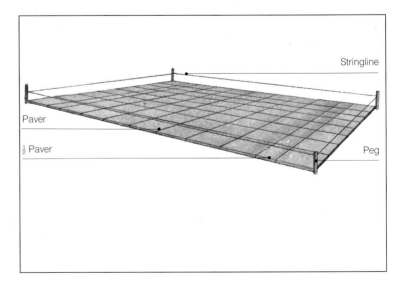

Stringline

Paver

½ Paver

Peg

FOUNDATION AND BASE

Lay out the site to be covered by the complete base using four corner pegs and a string line (fig. 1). Choose a sheltered part of the garden: this will minimize the risk of structural damage in storms and high winds.

Make sure you choose a flat site – sloping terrain would need a great deal of excavation work to enable a level base to be laid.

The base can be laid using either concrete pavers or poured concrete. If you choose pavers, then you will need 72 pavers measuring $24 \times 24 \times 1\frac{1}{2}$in ($600 \times 600 \times 38$mm). You will also need 16 half-size pavers (24×12in [600×300mm]). These are required to ensure that only a narrow border remains around the walls of the house while the joists rest centrally on the pavers (Base and Floor Assembly).

The pavers should be laid on a 1:5 mix of cement to sand. You need to build in a slope of $\frac{1}{4}$in per foot from front to back to ensure that rainwater drains away and does not lie alongside the joists and cause them to rot away.

Alternatively, if you use concrete you will have to dig out about 5in (125mm) of soil and lay a foundation of well-compacted gravel covered with a 2in (50mm) layer of concrete mixed from one part cement to five parts ballast.

You will have to set up a form (wooden frame) of lumber to retain the concrete, again having first staked out the site. The forms should be held in place using stakes driven into the ground. Old floorboards, or similar, are ideal for forms. Do not forget to build in a slight slope in the formwork from front to back.

When the base is completed you can lay out the joists. Use 2×4in (50×100mm) members for the floor joists, making sure that they have been thoroughly treated with preservative. Ideally, pressure-treated stock should be used. There are 13 joists in all, with a double row being support the end walls. The outer joists support the veranda floor at each end.

Each joist should be laid on a strip of bituminous felt to serve as a vapor barrier and to prevent moisture seeping up through the base. Since the base has a slight slope built into it from front to back, you will need to lay small shim pieces about every 24in (600mm) under each joist to bring it level. This is important since you want to have a level floor.

Next lay the summer garden house floor (fig. 3). This is $\frac{3}{4}$in (19mm) exterior-grade plywood and the area is nominally 12×8ft (3.6×2.4m). The sheets should be affixed to the joists using $1\frac{1}{2}$in (38mm) No. 8 screws at 16in (400mm) centers around the edge. Affix the middle sheet first and then a sheet either side, cut to fit as needed. Next lay $\frac{3}{4} \times 2$in (19×50mm) strips of plywood on which the front and back walls will sit.

The end joists, which support the veranda floor, can be removed temporarily since they will be a hazard while the summer garden house frame and roof are constructed.

② **Setting Out and Leveling Floor Joists**
Wood joists are laid down at 24in (600mm) centers. A double row is needed to support the end walls. Since the pavers are laid to a slight fall, shims are needed below the joists to level them.

③ **Laying the Plywood Floor**
The floor is formed from $\frac{3}{4}$in (19mm) thick exterior-grade plywood screwed to the floor joists using $1\frac{1}{2}$in No. 8 screws. Lay the middle panel first and then one other panel on each side.

Indicates fall required in slabs

Concrete paver

Joist

Shim

WALLS

The inner faces of the walls are made from $\frac{1}{2}$in (12mm) exterior-grade plywood. Cut out the pieces needed for each of the four walls. The window openings, front and back, are about $27\frac{1}{2} \times 23\frac{1}{2}$in (700 × 600mm) and the doorway is about 78 × 32in (2000 × 810mm). If you buy the door ready-made, then tailor the door opening to size – remember to allow for the dimensions of the door frame.

Taking each wall by turn, lay out the 2 × 2in (50 × 50mm) studding at the centers shown (fig. 1). Note also that the short horizontal blocking is intentionally slightly misaligned in order to stagger the screws in the wall panels.

Lay the plywood panels on the studding with the inside surface uppermost – these will form the internal walls of the house (fig. 2). Use $1\frac{1}{2}$in (38mm) No. 8 screws to secure the panels to the studs at 16in (400mm) intervals. Countersink and fill all of the screw heads.

The door and window openings are all framed with 1 × 2in (25 × 50mm) trimmers toe-nailed to the studs using 2in (50mm) nails.

The walls are joined together using 5in (125mm) long $\frac{1}{2}$in (12mm) diameter bolts. If you position all four walls (fig. 3) using a helper and temporary supporting struts, you can drill bolt holes at the corners through adjoining vertical studs. Clamp each corner before drilling the holes and securing the bolts, leaving a little "play" at this stage for final adjustment of the four walls. Four bolts are needed at each corner at the approximate positions indicated (fig. 1, back wall). The order of assembly is to form one corner with the front wall to one end wall and bolt together; then bolt the back wall to the other end wall; finally, bolt the two remaining corners together.

When all the walls have been joined and are square, the sole plates of each wall (fig. 2, front wall) can be nailed through to the joists using 4in (100mm) nails at about 16in (400mm) centers.

1 **Assembling Framework for each Wall**

The illustrations show the arrangement of the 2 × 2in (50 × 50mm) studding for each of the four walls. *Top* Front frame with allowance for the door and windows. *Middle* Rear frame with a window opening. *Below* Solid end walls.

Sole plate

WALL FRAME ASSEMBLY

2 **Adding Inner Walls to Frames**

The inner walls are formed from $\frac{1}{2}$in (12mm) thick plywood. The front wall is made from five pieces with cut-outs for the windows in the side sections. The sheets are affixed to the frame using $1\frac{1}{2}$in No. 8 screws.

3 **Joining the Four Frames Together**

Each studding framework is joined together using 5in (125mm) long bolts. Using a helper, supporting struts and clamps, keep the frames aligned at the corners. Drill holes for four bolts at each corner and bolt together.

SUMMER GARDEN HOUSE: ROOF ASSEMBLY

LAYOUT OF ROOF

WALL PLATE PURLIN

MAIN ROOF TRUSS

INTERMEDIATE PURLIN

SHORT CEILING JOIST

RIDGE PURLIN

PURLIN

RAISED ROOF PURLIN

END JACK RAFTER

CEILING JOIST

HIP RAFTER

EAVE PURLIN

40in   48in   48in   48in   40in

18ft 8in

SECTION ACROSS LENGTH OF ROOF

MAIN ROOF TRUSS

JACK RAFTER HEAD PLATE

SHORT CEILING RAFTER

POST

ROOF

The striking, veranda-covering roof of this summer garden house is a fundamental part of its design. It consists of a pitched roof clad with sheets of corrugated metal and with a "hip" at either end projecting out to cover the sides of the veranda. It is quite complicated, so it is strongly recommended that you spend a little while studying the plans, and then tackle the construction one step at a time as described here. The positions of the rafters and purlins will become much clearer as you start to put the pieces together.

MAIN TRUSSES

Start by making the four main roof trusses. Each truss, a triangular-shaped frame mitered at the top, is made from two 2 × 3in (50 × 75mm) angled rafters each about 8ft 8in (2.6m) long (allowing for them being overlong), reinforced with a triangular plywood gusset at the top, and braced with a ceiling joist at the appropriate level.

The rafters are cut at an angle at the top, butted together and held at the correct angle by being nailed to a ½in (12mm) thick triangular plywood gusset. Each triangular plywood gusset is pitched at 26°, and this controls the angle of all the rafters. The rafters are prevented from spreading by the ceiling joists, which are bolted to them toward the bases of the rafters.

All the main trusses are the same, except that the two end trusses have double rafters, formed by bolting pairs of rafters together using ½in (12mm) lag bolts with steel connectors on the bolts sandwiched between the two members. Similar bolts and connectors are used to bolt the ceiling joists to the rafters.

Ensure that the four main trusses are cut and nailed at the same angle: nail the first truss on a flat surface, and use this truss as a template for nailing subsequent trusses.

Make all the rafters about 8in (200mm) overlong; they can then be cut to the correct length after they have been installed. Nail the top furring in place.

AFFIXING MAIN TRUSSES

Lift the main trusses onto the walls, spacing them approximately 48in (1200mm) apart. Do not forget to position the double rafter trusses at each end. Make sure that all the trusses are square and vertical, and then nail them down to the top plates of the front and back walls, using 6in (150mm) round head nails which should be toe-nailed into the top plates (*see* **Techniques, page 151**).

Temporarily hold the trusses in place so that they are vertical: nail long boards diagonally across the rafters to act as bracing (fig. 1, below). Position the boards carefully so that there is enough room to affix the purlins at the ridge, wall plate, and eave levels.

AFFIXING PURLINS

Cut and affix the ridge purlins (horizontal members) in place. These are the same overall length as the front and back wall structure and are secured to the furring on either side of the apex of the main trusses.

Cut the eave purlins (positioned at the front and back to support the outermost edges of the pitched roof covering) 8ft 2in (2.5m) overlong to give an overhang of 49in (1250mm) at each end (fig. 2). Affix in place by nailing into rafters.

Next cut the front and back wall plate purlins (the ones above the eave purlins), approximately 25½in (650mm) overlong at each end to allow for trimming later. Nail in place on the rafters (fig. 2). Remove the diagonal bracing and cut and secure the two intermediate purlins (one each side) midway between the ridge and wall plate purlins. These butt up against the ends of the furring pieces, which should now be cut to length. The intermediate purlins are about 12in (300mm) overlong each end for cutting back at an angle later.

MAKING THE RAISED ROOF SECTION

The furring acts as a shim over the rafters. Fit a second purlin close to the lower end of the furring pieces to form the raised roof section.

---

1 **Construction of Main Roof Trusses**
Each truss is formed by nailing it to a pre-cut ½in (12mm) thick plywood gusset pitched at 26°, and then braced by a ceiling joist for stability. End trusses have double raters. After positioning, rafters are braced by purlins.

2 **Affixing the Purlins to the Roof Trusses**
With trusses spaced along the top plates on the walls, and held upright by temporary diagonal braces, cut and nail the ridge purlins in place. Note that eave, wall plate and intermediate purlins are left temporarily overlength.

Plywood gusset
Furring piece
Diagonal brace
Ceiling joist

Ridge purlin
Raised roof purlin
Intermediate purlin
Wall plate purlin
Eave purlin

SUMMER GARDEN HOUSE: ROOF ASSEMBLY

SETTING OUT HIP ROOF AT EACH END

Measure 39in (1000mm) along the top outer edge of the eave purlin, measuring from the outer face of the outside truss. Tack a line from this point (string will do) to where the end lean-to roof meets the end truss. This should form a roof pitch at the ends of about 36° (8½-in-12). Make up a triangle of plywood or scrap wood to this angle and use it to check the roof pitch during all stages of construction (fig. 2).

Tie another string line from the top of the first eave purlin (39in [1000mm] from the face of the end truss) to the top of the corresponding eave purlin on the opposite side (39in [1000mm] out from the end truss). From this point, take another string line up to where the end lean-to roof meets the end truss. With these string lines in place, 39in (1000mm) out from the end truss, the general arrangement of the roof hips and pitch down to eave level on the lean-to roofs at each end of the building will become apparent.

Cut the end jack rafters (four at each end) overlong, and also the short ceiling joists for the ends (again, four at each corner). Both are cut from 2 × 3in (50 × 75mm) stock (fig. 6).

Cut the jack rafter top plates (which support the jack rafters against the end trusses). Nail or bolt these to the end trusses as shown (fig. 3), and after affixing trim the ends of the top plates to the slope of the main roof rafters.

Use an adjustable T-bevel set to the angle required for the ends of the jack rafters where they butt against the end trusses, and trim the ends of the jack rafters to this angle. On the underside of each rafter cut a birdsmouth (notch) so that the rafter will sit neatly on the top plate. The eave ends are left overlong for the time being.

Nail the four jack rafters and the four short ceiling joists in place at each end. Check that the top of the rafters are aligned and slope in line with the previously set string guidelines. Make sure that the undersides of the short ceiling joists

are horizontal and are in line with the undersides of the ceiling joists at the front and back of the building.

Note that in the center of the ends there are two rafters set 3in (75mm) apart (fig. 4). Later these will be bolted to the central veranda support post.

Cut the 1 × 6in (25 × 125mm) hip rafters (boards) overlong and hold them as close to their final position as possible so that the correct angles can be marked on the ends of the front and rear purlins which rest against the hip boards and which are now cut to length. Again, an adjustable T-bevel is used to mark these angled cuts, which are angled in two directions to ensure that the ends of the purlins fit tightly against the hip rafters when these are affixed in place.

At the top, the hip rafter is notched to fit over the jack rafter top plate (fig. 3), and the end of the hip rafter is angled so that the hip rafter fits tightly against the main end truss. This angle needs careful marking with an adjustable T-bevel to ensure an accurate fit, particularly

of the support notch at the top end. The top surface of each hip rafter should be carefully lined up with the top of the purlins.

The hip rafters can now be fitted and held in place by nailing to the ends of the front and rear purlins.

Next, cut and fasten by nailing the three 2 × 3in (50 × 75mm) purlins on the lean-to roofs at the ends of the building. They must be cut to length and angled so that they butt tightly against the hip rafters at the ends, and align at the corner hips with the front and back purlins.

Cut and fit the 3 × 3in (75 × 75mm) veranda support posts in the middle of the end sections to fit between the concrete base and the twin central jack rafters. The base of each post should rest on a small piece of lead, which seals the end grain very effectively. Using connector plates and ½in (12mm) diameter lag bolts, drill and bolt to the floor joists at the base and between the twin jack rafters at the top. Leave overlong for the time being, and later trim flush, angled with the tops of the purlins.

---

1 **Cross-section of the Width Showing the Raised Roof Section**
Note how the furring pieces lift the ridge and raised roof purlins to create the raised roof section. Also look at the eave area and note how the truss ends are trimmed vertically, level with the front top edge of the eave purlin, to give a plumb fastening for the fascia board to which the gutters are affixed.

2 **Trimming the Rafter Ends**
Adjustable bevel marks rafter ends (shown without eave purlin). Use a template to check roof pitch.

Ridge purlin
Plywood gusset
Intermediate purlin
Wall plate purlin
Furring
Raised roof purlin
26°
Post
Eave purlin

Roof pitch template
36°

HIP ROOF ASSEMBLY

Detail 3

Detail 6

Detail 4

Detail 5

The 3 × 3in (75 × 75mm) corner veranda support posts fit between the concrete base and the top sides of the hip boards. Allow 1–1¼in (25–30mm) clearance from the eave purlins. The undersides of the hip rafters are notched to take posts, and the top ends of the posts are cut out with matching notches which allow them to be bolted to the hip rafters (fig. 5). Cut the post tops to the same angles as the roof pitches and to the level of the purlins.

FITTING FASCIA BOARDS

Use an adjustable T-bevel to mark the rafter ends with a vertical line where they will be trimmed. When the fascia boards are affixed onto the rafter ends they will be upright, allowing gutters to be fitted. Trim the rafters in line with the top of the eave purlin. The bottoms of the rafter ends are trimmed level with the bottom of the fascia boards, either before or after the fascias are secured. Also trim the ends of the hip rafters to take the fascia boards.

Cut the fascia boards from 1 × 6in (25 × 150mm) stock.

❸ Hip Board/Head Plate Join
Notch hip board to fit over jack rafter top plate. Angle board end to fit against truss. Purlins fit against hip.

❹ Intermediate Veranda Support Post
Posts bolt between central jack rafters. Saw tops level with purlins.

❺ Corner Post/Hip Board Join
Notch hip boards for corner posts, which are slotted to fit over hips. Bolt and trim tops to roof slope.

❻ Jack Rafters/Ceiling Joists
Underside view of the jack rafters nailed to short ceiling joists. Tops of rafters must align.

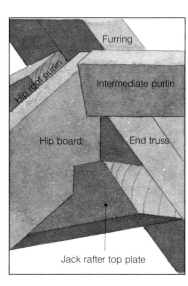

Furring

Hip roof purlin

Intermediate purlin

Hip board

End truss

Jack rafter top plate

Eave purlin

Jack rafter

Twin jack rafters

Intermediate post

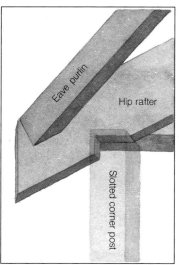

Eave purlin

Hip rafter

Slotted corner post

Purlin

Short ceiling joist

Jack rafter

Jack rafter top plate

Summer Garden House: Detailing

Fitting Corrugated Metal Roof

You can buy corrugated metal sheets cut to any size. Secure the lower sections first by nailing through the peaks of the corrugations into the purlins and screwing through the valleys using special self-sealing screws. Make sure that adjacent sheets overlap by at least two corrugations on each side of the panels.

Install flashing along the lower purlin of the raised roof sections and press the flashing down onto the lower roof sheets using a roller. Apply a similar strip of flashing from the main end trusses onto the end lean-to roof sheets (fig. 1). Nail ½in (12mm) bevel clapboards to the end trusses to form gable ends.

Finally, affix the raised-roof corrugated sheets, screwing and nailing (as above) into the furring pieces. Adjacent sheets must overlap at least two corrugations on both sides of each panel. Fit and fasten metal capping pieces to the ridge and hips of the hip roof sections.

1 Lower Roof Flashing
Lay flashing along the lower raised roof purlin; roll the flashing on to the lower roof sheets.

Detailing

With the main walls constructed and the roof in place, the final detailing jobs can be completed.

Between the wall studs on all four walls, fit 2in (50mm) thick fiberglass wall batts for insulation (fig. 4). The material is flexible and will need to be held in place by tapping brads or staples into the studs in much the same way that glass is held in a window frame.

The window and door frames are then cut to length from 1 × 5in (25 × 125mm) S4S (smooth 4 sides) softwood and temporarily screwed in place (figs. 2 and 3). Make up the window sashes from 2 × 2in (50 × 50mm) wood screwed together, and then nail through the outsides of the sashes to affix the glazing bars (these are stocked by lumberyards). Screw the sashes into the frames.

The exterior cladding can now be nailed in place on each wall, starting at the base and working upwards (fig. 4). Cut the clapboarding to fit neatly around the window frames and the door frame (see **Techniques, page 151**).

Cut and nail in place the 1 × 6in (25 × 150mm) fascia boards to the eaves and the 2 × 2in (50 × 50mm) rafter ties.

Corner boards are needed at the four corners of the summer garden house to close off the end grain of the exterior cladding. The boards should be cut to length and set temporarily in place.

Having checked everything over you can now start to decorate. Remove the corner boards while the exterior cladding is treated with exterior-grade preservative, stain, or paint, then paint the boards in a contrasting color before nailing them back in place.

The door and window frames can now be painted, along with the roof and fascia board.

Now secure the gutters, giving them a slight fall toward each corner, where a small hole should be cut. Secure a chain through each outlet and run it down to the ground to channel rain water into a drywell. Alternatively, you could fit a combined stopend and downspout outlet at each corner of the gutter; however, this will mean that you will not be able to run the chains down to the ground at the exact corners of the summer garden house – to the detriment of the overall design.

If the external joists were temporarily removed while the project was being built then re-lay them now on a strip of bituminous felt and secure them to the veranda support posts as described earlier (page 62).

The "duckboard" floor of the veranda is now formed by screwing

1 × 3in (25 × 75mm) boards to the joists leaving $\frac{3}{4}$in (19mm) spaces between them. Use 2in (50mm) long No. 8 screws.

The windows can now be glazed using $\frac{1}{8}$in (3mm) glass held in place with glazing bars pinned to the frame. It is important that the glazing bars are set square to each other so that the glass will slot comfortably in place. Check each "window" for square by measuring the diagonals, which should be equal. When ordering the glass, buy it about $\frac{1}{8}$in (2–3mm) smaller than the window opening, both in width and height, to allow for normal expansion.

If you prefer, you can buy a ready-made ledged and braced door; alternatively, you can make one using tongue-and-groove boards with 1 × 4in (25 × 100mm) wood for the ledges (cross rails) and braces (diagonals). The door can be full-length or a stable door as here. If you choose the latter, you simply make the two smaller doors with a lower rail for each one. In a full-length door, only one central rail will need to be fitted.

Plywood

Lining

Glass

Frame

Exterior cladding

Glazing bar

Glazing batten

2 Affixing the Door Head
Screw door lining to the studwork, with $\frac{1}{2}$ × 1in (12 × 25mm) doorstops nailed to sides and top of frame.

3 Window Frame Assembly
Above The top and bottom sections of the frame are fastened to the 1 × 5in (25 × 125mm) linings.

4 Exterior Cladding
Below Exterior walls are formed from overlapping boards nailed to the studwork; work from bottom up.

Stud

Door Stop

Door lining

SUMMER GARDEN HOUSE: DETAILING

A ledged and braced door is made by simply nailing the boards to the ledges and braces. It is constructed by laying the top and bottom rails on a flat surface and then screwing the tongue-and-groove boards to them (*see* **Techniques, page 151**). The boards should overlap the rails by about 1in (25mm) at either end.

The diagonal brace is then fitted by notching it into the ledges and, again, screwing through the door and into the brace. The purpose of the brace is to transmit the weight to the hinges and so prevent the door from sagging. It is important that the braces are affixed the right way around (*see* Door Assembly, fig. 1).

Use two butt hinges to hang each door. These are affixed to the end grain of the rails. If you make a framed door then also use butt hinges: two 3in (75mm) sizes for each half of a stable door, or three for a full-length door.

Next, fit the $\frac{1}{2} \times$ 1in (12 × 25mm) door stops – two vertical pieces and a horizontal top piece – to the door frame (fig. 2, page 65). These stops must be positioned accurately: hold the door in place and mark the positions of the stops immediately inside its closed position. This ensures that the stops are fitted accurately. Here, they are positioned about 1in (25mm) back from the front of the door frame.

Complete the interior by cladding the ceiling using tongue-and-groove boards, not forgetting to insert fiberglass insulating batts between the joists (fig. 2), held in place by brads as with the walls. The interior walls can be decorated according to your requirements using exterior paint, varnish stain, or microporous paint.

Finally, at each corner, dig a 12 × 12 × 12in (300 × 300 × 300mm) drywell and fill with gravel or pebbles (fig. 3). Embed the ends of the chains into them so that they are held tautly in place.

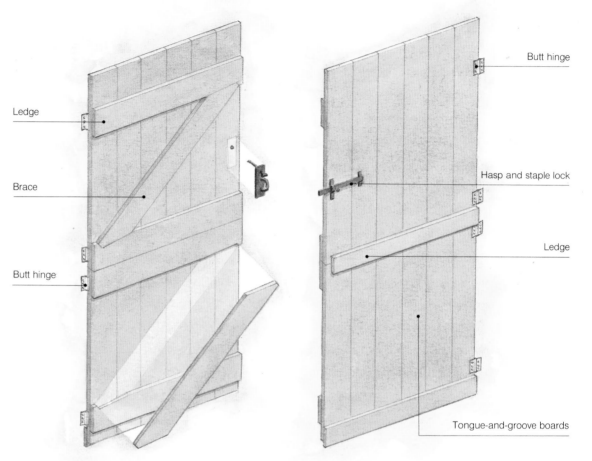

Ledge

Brace

Butt hinge

Butt hinge

Hasp and staple lock

Ledge

Tongue-and-groove boards

1 Door Assembly
Above **The ledged and braced door can either be a stable door (as shown) or a single unit.**

2 Insulating the Ceiling
Clad the ceiling with tongue-and-groove boards, and place insulating batts between the joists.

3 Making the Drywells
A chain conducts rainwater from the gutters to a drywell – a hole filled with shingle or pebbles.

DEN . . . GAZEBO . . . HIDEAWAY . . . CHALET . . . SHANTY . . . BOTHY . . . HUNTING BOX . . . CROFT . . . PAD . . . OUTHOUSE . . .

SHACK . . . PLAYHOUSE . . . SNUG . . . CABIN . . . SHED . . . BOLT HOLE . . . STUDIO . . . PAVILION . . . LODGE . . . RETREAT . . .

POTTING SHED . . . HUT . . . SANCTUARY . . . HIDEY-HOLE . . . CUBBYHOLE . . . HAVEN . . . GARDEN ROOM . . . .

SUMMER GARDEN HOUSE

A CHANGE OF SCENERY

In a secluded part of the garden, the summer garden house can be used as a simple retreat. The interior is large enough to function as a tool room and potting shed (right) or as a cozy study (opposite).

PLAYHOUSE

A HOME OF THEIR OWN

*Whether as a private den away from their parents or as a "real home"
on a miniature scale, a playhouse in the garden will give children
hours of fun and laughter.*

A playhouse in the garden will
attract children like bees to a honey-
pot. Playhouses are excellent for
developing children's learning skills,
encouraging them to exercise their
imaginations. As they play with other
children, they will develop inter-
personal skills at the same time as
enjoying hours of fun. Depending
on the age of your children, you can
decorate the interior for them, or
encourage them to equip it and
paint it themselves. In the latter case,
make sure that they only use non-
toxic paints, which should also be
washable, so that the walls can be
painted time and again.

By keeping internal fixtures to a
minimum, the children can use the
playhouse to represent a variety of
structures: from a hospital to a shop,
an adult living room to an office, or
as a den away from the grown-ups.

When children finally outgrow the
playhouse, it can be adapted without too much expenditure or alte-
ration for use as storage space for
garden equipment.

The model shown in the photograph is situated in the grounds of
Castle Drogo, a Lutyens house near
Exeter in the west of England admi-
nistered by the National Trust. The
playhouse was built *circa* 1909 as a
birthday present and was transferred to its present home from a
house in Sussex *circa* 1928.

Our plans show how a playhouse
of a similar style could be constructed. For all the framing use
1½ × 1½in (38 × 38mm) S4S (smooth
4 sides) softwood, as accuracy is
important. All the relevant dimensions are shown on the illustrations.
Glued and nailed butt joints are
used throughout.

PLAYHOUSE ASSEMBLY

FRONT

60in

54in

54in

30in

19in

10in

33in

48in

SIDE

PLAYHOUSE

BASE

A solid, level base is essential; otherwise it will not be possible to build the house. The simplest method is to lay concrete pavers on sand. To prevent damp in the soil creeping up and attacking the floor, lay a polyethylene membrane below the sand as a vapor barrier.

The base should be made slightly smaller than the house so that the wall cladding extends just beyond it all around. This means that rainwater running down the walls will not trickle inside the house, but will instead drip onto the ground.

The overall area of the house is 54 × 48in (1370 × 1220mm) and the base is $\frac{1}{4}$in (5mm) less all round at 53$\frac{1}{2}$ × 47$\frac{1}{2}$in (1360 × 1210mm). The floor itself is constructed as a normal house floor with floorboards nailed at right angles to joists. For the joists, use 1 × 2in (25 × 50mm) rough sawn wood. Five joists running from front to back will be sufficient. The two end joists are just inside the ends of the floorboards, with the other three spaced equally between.

The floorboards can be square edged or tongue-and-groove. The former simply butt up to each other, while tongue-and-groove boards interlock. You can use either 4in (100mm) or 5in (125mm) wide boards for the floor; thicknesses range from $\frac{1}{2}$–1$\frac{1}{4}$in (12–32mm), but buy the thinnest available.

Lay the five joists on the ground, then nail one end board at right angles to each joist. Repeat for the other side. Use 2in (50mm) finishing nails and punch the heads below the surface.

At this point, the floor will be held solidly in position so that you can add more boards, making sure that square edge boards butt up closely and that tongue-and-groove boards are tightly interlocked. You will probably have to remove the last board, affixed earlier, to trim it to size before reinstalling it.

WALLS

Affix $\frac{3}{4}$in (19mm) thick marine plywood over the wall framing. The front of the house is split into two separate frames with the door in the middle. The two frames are identical with allowance made for a window on either side. The windows can be any size provided that they look right proportionately – here, 12in square (300mm square) is about right.

The top horizontal member holds the two frames together, but until the side and back frames are added it will be flimsy. So, as a temporary support, add a strut across the doorway as shown (fig. 1). This can be nailed in place and removed when the frames have been joined and the wall panels added.

Light through the front windows is unlikely to be sufficient: a window up to 20 × 16in (500 × 380mm) can be built into the rear wall.

The side walls are plain. Use a top and bottom horizontal member for rigidity and to strengthen each plywood wall panel.

ASSEMBLING THE WALLS

The front and back wall frames are screwed to the base using 3in (75mm) No. 8 screws. This is especially vital in exposed locations where high wind could easily turn the house over. The horizontal members on each side are now affixed, together with the central supports.

The plywood wall panels can now be cut to size and nailed to the frames using 1$\frac{1}{2}$in (38mm) nails, again punching the heads below the surface. When these are in place, the house will be very solid. Remember to cut the panels to extend just below the base.

ROOF

First fix the roof dormer in position. This is made from two A-shaped frames joined with a glued miter joint and reinforced with two 1$\frac{1}{2}$in (38mm) corrugated fasteners. Plywood offcuts nailed in place strengthen the roof-to-wall joints and reinforce the miter joint at the apex of the A-frame, while a batten the length of the side wall frames runs between them at the apex. These frames are then clad with bevel clapboards, nailed in place with 2in (50mm) finishing nails.

Start at the bottom and work up to the ridge. The boards are nailed

① Constructing the Front Frame
Build all of the frames from 1$\frac{1}{2}$ × 1$\frac{1}{2}$in (38 × 38mm) S4S softwood. Brace the opening for the door at the front and allow for a window on either side. Roof dormer frame rests centrally on top.

② Constructing the Back Frame
The back frame is a very simple construction of glued and nailed butt joints. A central window can be fitted at the back to improve the amount of light inside the playhouse.

with the thinner edge uppermost so that the thicker edge of the board above overlaps it by $\frac{1}{2}$in (12mm) (*see* **Techniques, page 151**).

At the top, you will probably have to trim the last board to fit. The ridge is sealed by using self-adhesive aluminum flashing tape. Cut the strip to the required length from the roll, peel back a little of the backing paper and position the tape on the roof. Press the tape into place with a cloth, peel back more of the backing paper and continue in this manner until the ridge is covered. Do not peel away all of the backing paper at once – the adhesive is powerful and will start to stick itself to the roof in the wrong place. Add two triangular plywood panels to enclose each end of the dormer. These are inset into the A-frames and glued in place using an epoxy resin.

When the dormer is complete it can be lifted into place and screwed and glued in place to the top of the wall frames.

The main roof is constructed similarly except that the A-frames are screwed in place and then the bevel clapboarding, cutting it to fit around the dormer as necessary.

Use plywood offcuts to strengthen the joints as before, and use triangular plywood panels inset into the A-frames and glued in place at either end.

WINDOWS

You have a choice for the windows: you can either use plain acrylic, or else you can decorate it with self-adhesive strips as imitation leaded lights. A similar effect can be achieved with self-adhesive black tape. An alternative is to use thin battens to form small "windows" within the main frame. For safety reasons, do not use glass.

DOOR

Construct the door from floorboards and affix two 1 × 4in (25 × 100mm) boards horizontally to serve as bracing and to prevent the door warping. Alternatively, you can use shiplap cladding smooth side out, which will give slightly better weather resistance (*see* **Materials, page 146**).

CHIMNEY

The chimney is optional. Make it from plywood offcuts joined with 1in square (25mm square) plywood strips in each corner, or use plastic joint blocks. A piece of plastic pipe forms the pot.

PAINTING

Before painting, all the wood which the children will be able to touch should be very carefully smoothed by sanding it down with a power sander to remove any splinters.

Use masonry paint for the main walls and treat the door with primer, undercoat, and exterior gloss. Coat the floor with an appropriate wood dye and exterior-grade varnish or a varnish stain; alternatively, it can be painted with masonry paint.

GUTTERS AND PIPES

The gutters and drainpipes are purely decorative. Use offcuts of plastic guttering – the smallest section made for sheds will do. Make the drainpipes from waste pipe held in place with pipe clips.

③ Constructing the Roof Dormer Frame
Reinforce the A-shaped frames with plywood offcuts at the apex. Additional plywood offcuts strengthen the roof-to-wall joints at the front and back. A batten the length of the side walls runs between the A-frames.

④ Making the Door
Make door from floorboards braced top and bottom. Weather bar at bottom throws rain clear of base.

⑤ Making the Chimney
This is purely decorative. Angle the plywood to sit on the apex of the roof. Add plastic pipe to form pot.

RABBIT RUN

RUN RABBIT, RUN
Pet rabbits can exercise in safety if you build a rabbit run. The dimensions can be adjusted according to the size and number of rabbits. The enclosed end section provides shelter in bad weather.

An enclosed run such as this will provide your rabbits with an area for safe daytime exercise. One section of the run is fully enclosed for occasions when the weather turns nasty. Be sure to anchor the run firmly to the ground to ensure that the rabbits cannot escape.

Treat all the wood with a good quality, non-toxic wood preservative that will not harm your rabbits and allow it to dry thoroughly before you start assembly. For the side cladding panels use $\frac{1}{4}$in (6mm) thick exterior-grade plywood; use the same material for the doors, but use $\frac{3}{8}$in (9mm) thickness for the floor.

Make up four A-shaped frames using 1 × 2in (25 × 50mm) softwood and strengthen them with 1 × 1in (25 × 25mm) cross pieces. The apex of each frame needs to be mitered and this joint can be

secured with a 1in (25mm) wide corrugated fastener. The other joints are secured using 1$\frac{1}{2}$in (38mm) No. 8 galvanized screws. Use waterproof adhesive on all joints.

Position the frames at 24in (600mm) spacings, then link them at either side with 72in (1800mm) lengths of $\frac{1}{4}$ × 1$\frac{1}{2}$in (6 × 38mm) plywood battens, top and bottom, attached using 1in (25mm) No. 8 screws driven into the A-frames.

Add the floor to the section that will be beneath the side cladding panels, pinning it to the two cross rails at the bottom of the A-frames with 1in (25mm) panel pins.

Use $\frac{1}{2}$in (12mm) plastic-coated wire mesh, which should be cut to finish 2in (50mm) inside the position of the plywood side panels. Use $\frac{3}{4}$in (19mm) staples to secure it to the frame of the run and secure it very strongly with staples at 3in (75mm) intervals. Cut out a triangle of mesh for the back frame of the run and secure it in the same way as for the sides. Nail the side panels in place on the frame, enclosing the edges of the mesh. The frame battens will create a small gap between the A-frame and the panels – add a filler piece if you want the panels flush.

The outer door should be cut out to sit snugly inside the end frame. Add small spacer blocks to bring it flush with the frame, then add a turnbutton for each corner to hold it in place. Make a turnbutton from a scrap piece of the $\frac{1}{4}$in (6mm) plywood and a 1in (25mm) No. 8 screw. Drill $\frac{1}{2}$in (12mm) ventilation holes in the door and nail a spare piece of wood to act as a handle.

The internal door is nailed in place inside the rabbit run to give access between the covered and uncovered sections. Drill $\frac{1}{2}$in (12mm) ventilation holes and cut the entrance with a saber saw.

Add a cap of building paper and shingles to seal the apex of the roof. Use bitumen-based adhesive to attach it.

RABBIT RUN ASSEMBLY

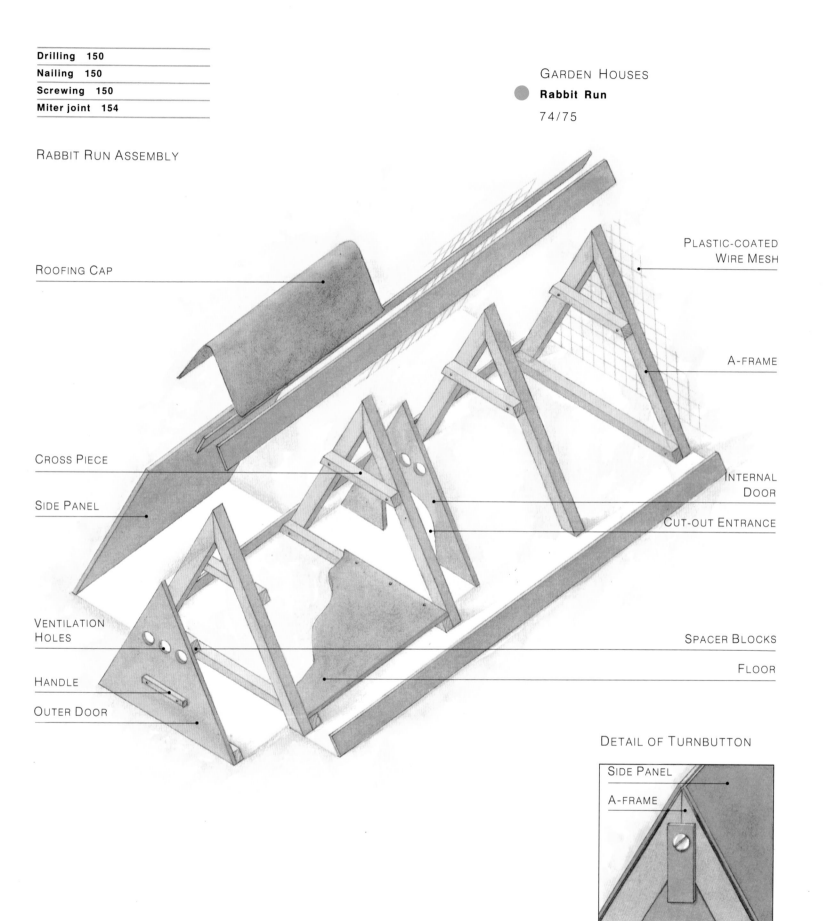

ROOFING CAP

PLASTIC-COATED WIRE MESH

A-FRAME

CROSS PIECE

INTERNAL DOOR

SIDE PANEL

CUT-OUT ENTRANCE

VENTILATION HOLES

SPACER BLOCKS

FLOOR

HANDLE

OUTER DOOR

DETAIL OF TURNBUTTON

SIDE PANEL

A-FRAME

BIRDHOUSE

The introduction of a birdhouse into your garden will help to conserve bird life and provide entertainment for the family. Given time, the birds will gain in confidence and come closer to your home.

The sizes given for this particular box (similar to the one in the photograph) are not critical so they can be altered by 1–2in (25–50mm) if preferred. The only thing that must be specific is the diameter of the entrance hole since this will govern the species of bird that will be encouraged to nest. The height that the box is sited above the ground is also important, but is generally not as critical as that of the entrance hole. A table of entrance hole diameters and above-ground heights is given opposite.

Rough-sawn wood is ideal for boxes, and a thickness of $\frac{5}{8}$in (16mm) makes joining easy. All joints are butted, and secured with waterproof wood adhesive and galvanized or alloy nails. Wood is a good insulator against heat and cold, it resists condensation, and blends well with any environment.

First, cut out the two side pieces, each measuring $4\frac{3}{4} \times 8$in (120 × 200mm). Next, cut a groove along the inside front edge of both pieces to serve as a channel for the door to slide in. The channels must be perfectly aligned; laying out, therefore, must be very accurate.

If you have a router then the channels can be cut out quickly and precisely using a straight-sided router bit. If you do not have a router then use a marking knife to scribe the edge of the groove. Next, use a back saw to cut the groove to the required depth along each edge before paring out the waste with a chisel. Work slowly and carefully until the sides and base of the channels are flat.

The back panel is a complete piece, shaped to support the roof panels. In position, it is slightly inset between the side panels.

The front is constructed from two separate pieces. The top triangular section is secured to the roof and has a hole of the required diameter drilled through it. The hole can be drilled using either an auger bit or, if you have one, an expansive bit fitted in a bit brace.

Should you not have a bit suitable for cutting large diameter holes then use a compass saw or a saber saw. First, drill a hole inside the outline of the hole to leave a starting position for the saw blade. Drill the hole with a normal twist drill. Cut out the shape and finish by sanding the edges (see **Techniques, page 149**).

The door is cut to dimensions of $6\frac{1}{2} \times 8$in (160 × 200mm). A rabbet is taken from each side so that the door sits neatly in the side panels.

The rabbet is cut easily with a router and straight-sided bit or with a back saw and chisel (see **Techniques, page 150**).

The roof is comprised of two panels; each panel measures $6 \times 8\frac{1}{2}$in (155 × 215mm). The roof is joined at the top using a miter joint. The joint, as throughout, is glued but this time it is secured with a 1in (25mm) corrugated fastener, tapped home flush with the surface.

When all the pieces have been cut to size, treat the exterior faces and edges only with a water-based wood preservative. It is best to leave internal faces untreated to avoid any toxic risk to the birds.

To assemble the birdhouse, first join the two side panels to the floor and then add the back panel.

Make up the roof, including the triangular front section, and attach this to the lower part.

Finally, with the sliding door in the closed position, drill a hole through either side of the birdhouse and into the door to a depth of 1in (25mm). Insert a 2in (50mm) galvanized steel nail into each hole to hold the door in place. The holes should be of a diameter to give the nails a tight but sliding fit.

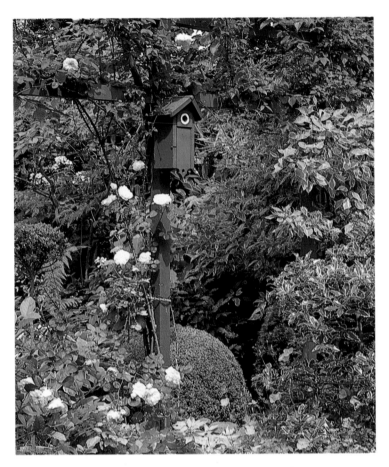

BACK YARD BIRD-LIFE

A birdhouse provides a safe haven for small birds and their young. By encouraging birds to nest in your garden, you will derive personal satisfaction and the enjoyment of observing wildlife close at hand.

Siting is not crucial, although a location within view of your house is obviously desirable for the family's enjoyment. Try to avoid anywhere where water is likely to cascade down, and, if your garden is exposed, position the birdhouse on the most sheltered side to avoid strong winds. Most birds prefer a direct flight line to the entrance.

If you are lucky, the birdhouse may lodge conveniently in the fork of a tree, but in most cases some form of attachment will be required. The simplest way is to secure plastic-coated garden wire to the back of the house using fencing staples, and then to wire the house to a tree trunk. With an immature tree, attach the wire fairly loosely to allow for growth of the trunk. It is best not to nail or screw directly into the tree as this may damage it.

Alternatively, you can place the birdhouse on top of a post. Sink a post support into the ground at the chosen site and insert a 4 × 4in (100 × 100mm) post cut to the appropriate height (see **Techniques, page 152**). Remove the sliding door from the birdhouse, drill a pilot hole through the base and into the post, and screw in place.

Remember to clear out the birdhouse annually, after the fledglings and their parents have flown.

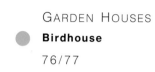
BIRDHOUSE ASSEMBLY

SPECIES	HOLE DIAMETER	HEIGHT ABOVE GROUND
TITMOUSE	1in (25mm)	6–15ft (2–5m)
NUTHATCH	1¼in (32mm)	12–15ft (4–5m)
TREE SPARROW	1¼in (32mm)	12–15ft (4–5m)

PART 3

PATIOS, PATHS, AND PONDS

The contrast between various garden surfaces – hard and soft, paved, turfed, planted, or water-filled – gives a garden its fundamental shape and design. Considerations such as where to build a patio or a flight of steps, which area to link with paths, or how to edge a flowerbed are not details to be decided piecemeal but basic issues which should be resolved at the outset.

All gardens, even informal ones, need some hard surfaces. Modern gardens are generally small and demands on the space available are high. One of our most important requirements today is that the garden should function as an extension of the house, as an outdoor room, which usually means that there must be some sort of paved seating area for relaxation. And there will always be the need for paths to connect one part of the garden to another, as a practical surface for walking and tending beds, and visually to divide flowerbeds from the lawn. Wherever possible, construct hard surfaces from natural materials that weather and age, and allow plants or grass to grow in the crevices of paving and paths, softening the edges so that these areas blend harmoniously with the rest of the garden.

PATIOS, PATHS, AND PONDS

Because hard surfaces are relatively expensive, fairly permanent, and take time and effort to install, it is critically important to work out your ideas on paper first. This is also the stage at which to plan changes of level or to work out how to accommodate an existing slope in the form of steps or terraces. Look at the shapes – the overall pattern – that the paved areas will create. Make sure that paths do not leave useless margins of lawn or awkward-shaped flowerbeds. Plan the connections so that the paths really go somewhere, rather than meander aimlessly. Establish the basic proportion of patio to lawn so that the paving reinforces the overall design of the garden. A formal layout, for example, usually relies on a strong, symmetrical grid which can be expressed in a higher proportion of paths and paved areas. In an urban garden, you may decide to dispense with a lawn altogether and work out a series of connecting paved areas and raised beds.

The range of materials suitable for hard surfacing is so great that there really is no need to rely solely on concrete. All the natural materials are much more sympathetic in the garden and they not only work well with plants but also with each other, so that you can mix materials to create interesting contrasts of texture and pattern. Bricks can be laid to create herringbone or basketweave patterns as well as simple coursing; be sure to choose frost-proof varieties for outdoor use and avoid ugly stock bricks which never weather. Stone – including bluestone, slate, and granite slabs – is traditional and expensive but can sometimes be reclaimed much more cheaply from building sites or builders' yards. Gravel can be rather dull; pebble paths are much more positive. Sea pebbles, in particular, set into concrete look wonderful laid in a mosaic. Treated wood is an excellent

garden material. Railway ties, which have a uniform thickness and are already treated against rot, can be put to a number of uses, from making steps, to forming the sides of raised beds. Slices can be cut from the trunks of fallen trees, treated, and used end grain-on for paths, steps, and patios. Decking, as a terrace or around the perimeter of a pond, is contemporary-looking and absorbs the heat of the sun to make a warm, comfortable surface.

Whatever material you choose will probably depend to a large extent on the amount of money you can spend, but try to form some kind of connection with the overall style of the house and the materials from which it is built. This is an important consideration, particularly for terraces or patios that immediately adjoin the house and create a relatively large surface area which has an impact on how the house is viewed.

If you cannot avoid the use of concrete, there are many ways of improving its rather dull and uniform appearance. Pavers are much better than a poured concrete slab and can be enormously improved if, instead of setting them in cement, they are laid with gaps in between. You can then fill the gaps with pebbles or plants such as creeping thyme or camomile to soften the edges. Choose pavers of a neutral shade and let color come from lichens and mosses: you can encourage lichen to grow by treating concrete with nonpasteurized milk or houseplant food. Even if most of the paving is concrete, an edging of brick or another more harmonious material will lift it out of the ordinary.

A path makes a good edge for a flowerbed or herbaceous border, separating planted areas from lawn and making mowing easier. In the absence of a path, beds need some form of containment. Conventional edging includes brick,

OUTDOOR FLOORING

The surfaces you choose for outdoor flooring can reinforce the overall style and design of the garden. A regular gridded pattern of smooth stone slabs suits the modern formal style of an urban garden (above). Decking is particularly sympathetic surrounding the perimeter of a pool, where it makes a comfortable surface for bare feet (above right). Slate tiles create a sleek paved area in an urban garden (above far right). For a more informal, country setting, a sweep of large cobblestone makes an attractive paved area (below right).

PATIOS, PATHS, AND PONDS

looped wire which also serves to prop up plants, and concrete bricks. Traditional terracotta edging, particularly the Victorian rope design, is also available. Less conventionally, you can make effective edging with whatever comes to hand: slivers of stone, old roofing slates, or thin horizontal slats of treated hardwood nailed to posts.

Water is one of the most delightful of all the elements in garden design, providing another contrast of surface, and retaining its interest even in winter when the garden is bare. A sheet of water, reflecting the sky, has always been a feature of formal designs; surrounded by moisture-loving plants and filled with fish and lily pads, a pond can come close to fulfilling everyone's dream of having a river running through the garden. Moving water – a jet, a fountain, a cascade, or a water sculpture – adds another dimension: sound. The tinkling noise of running water in the garden is extremely pleasant and restful.

There are also good, practical reasons for incorporating water into a garden design. A pond or pool provides a supply of water at air temperature, which presents far less of a shock to young seedlings than water from a hose. Even in a dry

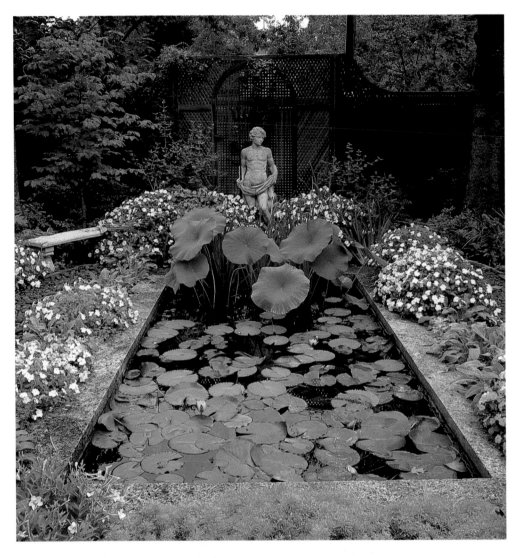

COOL WATER
Formal pools of water can be incorporated into even the smallest garden (right and above right), although pools designed to look like natural lakes need more space around them to be successful.

SURFACE INTEREST
A contrast of different surfaces – terracotta, stone, brick, or concrete – enlivens a garden design (opposite and above opposite.).

area, a pond will create its own microclimate where you can grow species such as arum lilies, irises, and other plants which flourish in damp conditions. And you do not have to stock your pond with fish for it to be attractive to insects, butterflies, and other wildlife.

In whatever form, water is a natural focal point in the garden. If the garden slopes, it is a simple proposition to create channels where water flows down the incline and collects in a pool, to be pumped back by an inexpensive recirculating pump. In hot countries, water in channels or running down stepped terraces has long been a means both of irrigating vegetable crops and, in courtyard gardens, of cooling the air. A still pool of water in a geometric shape is often the centerpiece of a formal garden, and formal cascades, for example, were an important feature of Italian Renaissance gardens. Sunken or raised pools in rectangular, circular, square, or L-shapes are relatively easy to build from concrete block with waterproof facing, the edges softened by clumps of rushes and irises. And in a small urban garden, the suggestion of water can be created very simply by the addition of a water sculpture. Water falling over large urns, slabs of stone, or boulders is much more effective and attractive than a waterfall or fountain which involves a contrived, rather crudely cast garden ornament.

Informal ponds and pools, where the intention is to create as natural an effect as possible, demand a larger garden to be successful. Groups of boulders, wooden decking, dense perimeter planting, and perhaps a flat, low bridge can give an informal pond a Japanese quality. Water on this kind of scale demands more attention and general maintenance than a simple formal pool if it is to be convincing and appealing.

WATER SCULPTURE

The delightful sound of running water in the garden is especially restful and pleasing. A water sculpture can be made very simply and economically, requiring only a minimal outlay for a small pump and the careful installation of a power supply.

This fountain consists of a large ribbed terracotta pot set into a pool which is in turn sunk into the ground and overhung with a brick surround. The dimensions of the pool have been calculated using standard bricks as a module.

A black polyethylene pond liner is fitted inside the pool and bricks and a tile make a central platform on which the pot rests. A waterproof power cable runs from the pump through a special conduit to connect with the main power source. A word of caution: special care must be taken to ensure that there is no leaking where the cable exits from the pool. It is also vital to lay the correct conduit for the cable so that it cannot be accidentally cut when digging above it.

An earthenware pot makes the best choice for the sculpture since terracotta is easier to drill than stoneware. A copper pipe is inserted through a hole drilled in the base of the pot. When the pool is filled with water, the pump sends a jet of water up through the pipe to fill the pot and overflow down the sides.

During the winter months, the power supply should be switched off and the pot emptied to prevent the risk of it being cracked by a hard frost.

WATER SCULPTURE

The sight and sound of moving water are among the most pleasurable experiences to be had in a garden on a hot summer's day. You need not go to the trouble and expense of installing an elaborate pond complete with waterfall, fish, and plants to enjoy this in your own garden – you can build a simple yet very effective water sculpture. The size of the pool is entirely optional, as is the centerpiece. We chose a pot with ridged sides since it gives an interesting surface for the water to splash onto and run down.

A submersible pump pushes the water up and out of the pot. Because the pump is electrically operated from the service at the house, it makes sense to keep the water sculpture as close to the house as possible; this saves having to run the buried cable a long distance. The submersible pump can be hidden beneath the pot or in a corner of the pond, covered by pond weed or water lilies.

With any water feature in the garden, safety must be paramount: a child can drown even in shallow water. If you have children and choose to install a pool then do make sure that it is made child-proof.

BUILDING THE POOL

Choose a level site and mark out the ground using a string line and pegs or a hose. This will give you a good idea of whether the position and size is satisfactory. Our pool is 39in square (1000mm square).

Dig out the hole to a depth of about 12in (300mm). The four sides should be tapered outward slightly and the base should be flat.

Cut out four pieces of exterior-grade plywood to form the pool sides. The top edge of the plywood should align with the level of the surrounding soil once you have cut around the edge of the pool to bed the brick or stone surround which will lie flush and overlap the edge of

TOOLS

SMALL CROSSCUT SAW

SPADE

CARPENTER'S LEVEL

SANDING BLOCK and SANDPAPER

STEEL BENCH RULE

TROWEL (if paving laid on mortar)

MALLET

POWER DRILL

ADJUSTABLE WRENCH

HACKSAW

SCREWDRIVER

MATERIALS

Part	Quantity	Material	Length
POT	1	Terracotta	As required
TUBE	1	$\frac{1}{2}$in (12mm) copper tubing	Height of pot
TILE	1	Terracotta	12 × 12in (300 × 300mm)
PAVING SLAB	1	Concrete	24 × 24in (600 × 600mm)
SIDES OF POOL	4	$\frac{3}{4}$in (19mm) shuttering plywood	As required

Also required: 1 submersible pump and outdoor cable; $\frac{1}{2}$in (12mm) compression tank outlet; clip and rubber washers; PVC or butyl pond liner; sand for lining pond; bricks for supporting terracotta tile and for pool surround; sand or soil for setting brick surround

the pool slightly. In our case, the plywood was 8$\frac{3}{4}$in (220mm) deep. Sand the plywood pieces to remove splinters and place in position.

Set a concrete paver in the middle. If you lay it on sand it will be simple to level. Lay a sand screed across the excavation, covering the paver by about $\frac{1}{2}$in (12mm).

The brick or paved surround will be far more appealing if weathered, second-hand material is used. Dig out the area around the pool to the width and depth required for the bricks or pavers being used. In our case, the area was 15in (375mm) wide all round to allow for a double row of 8in (200mm) bricks overlapping the pond edge by 1in (25mm). The depth was approximately 3in (75mm) to allow for the 2$\frac{1}{4}$in (60mm) brick depth plus a $\frac{5}{8}$in (15mm) layer of fine soil or sand underneath. If you lay the bricks so that they will be level with the lawn, mowing will be easier.

FITTING THE LINER

The length of liner equals twice the pool depth plus the overall length of the pool (including the brick surround); the width of liner should be twice the depth of the pool plus the overall width.

Lay the pond liner in place following the manufacturer's instructions. Allow the excess edges of the liner to lap up over the sides of the pond, then weight it down temporarily with bricks while the pond is being filled. The weight of the water will gradually force the liner to stretch to the shape of the plywood walls. Check with the instructions as to how long you should allow the liner to stretch until it will be smooth.

Remove the temporary bricks and trim the liner to leave an overlap of about 6in (150mm) to lie below the brick surround.

Next, lay the bricks. Lay the course surrounding the edge of the pool first so that the bricks will overlap the water by 1in (25mm). It is a good idea to lay the corner bricks first and then to rest a straight-edge and carpenter's level across them; bring them level by adjusting the bed of sand or fine soil below and tapping each brick with the shaft of a mallet. It is then easy to fill in the remaining bricks, leveling each one with neighboring bricks, and filling in the gaps with sand or soil so that plants and moss can grow up in the cracks. Although reasonable alignment of the bricks is important, second-hand bricks can tend to be

slightly off center, but that gives the surround a rustic charm. However, it is important that the surface is level so that no one will trip. Note the brick arrangement used to turn the corners (fig. 1).

PREPARING THE POT

The base of the pot sits on a 12in square (300mm square) terracotta tile, itself supported by two leveled bricks, laid on edge and spaced at the required distance (fig. 2). The water level should be slightly above the tile so that the bottom of the pot is just submerged. The pump is placed below the tile.

Drill a $\frac{3}{4}$in (19mm) diameter hole through the center of the base of the pot to take a $\frac{1}{2}$in (12mm) tank outlet fitting. Use a carbide drill bit at slow speed. A larger hole is needed in the tile to take the pipe from the pump; to make this, drill a series of small holes closely together in a circle. As the small holes are joined up, a larger hole will be formed.

FITTING THE PUMP

Fit the compression tank outlet through the holes in the pot and tile ensuring that rubber washers are used on both sides and that the nuts are not overtightened; otherwise the pot could crack. Using a hacksaw, cut a length of copper tube to extend from inside the compression joint to the rim of the pot (fig. 3).

Attach the rubber tube from the pump to the compression outlet, if necessary using a clip to secure it. If the base of the pot is too thick then there might not be sufficient thread left to attach the tube. If so, screw on an extension piece.

The pump is powered from the house electrical service. It can be operated directly from the main but it is safer to feed it back through a transformer situated in the house which makes the supply low voltage for safety but adequate to power a pump. The cable should be armored for outdoor use and laid in a plastic conduit underground and fed into the pool from below the brick surround. There will be local regulations about this, so check first.

You can then switch on the power supply to the pump and enjoy the results. It is a good idea to remove the pot and store it inside during the winter as it may crack in freezing weather.

WATER SCULPTURE ASSEMBLY

COPPER TUBE

TERRACOTTA POT

CABLE FROM PUMP

BRICK SUPPORT

POND LINER

PLYWOOD

CONCRETE PAVER

SAND

PUMP

TERRACOTTA TILE

OUTLET

TRANSFORMER

① **Detail of Brick Surround**
At each corner of the surround the bricks are laid in pairs perpendicular to the adjoining pair.

② **Terracotta Pot Support**
Pot rests on tile supported by two bricks. Copper tube is connected to pump through holes in pot and tile.

③ **Connecting Pump to Pot**
Pump pipe is connected to copper tube by compression tank outlet which feeds through pot and tile.

Copper tube

Tile

Pump

Cable feed

Compression joint

Rubber washer

Base of pot

Clip

Tile

Rubber pipe

PLANT STAND

This elegant, rectilinear plant stand, or jardiniere, is inspired by the work of the early twentieth-century designer Josef Hoffmann (1870–1956). He was a Viennese architect, a founding member of the Wiener Werkstätte and a pioneer of functional design. His furniture displays a lack of embellishment and an interest in proportion that was developed further by designers of the Modernist Movement.

Essentially a simple structure, it is made slightly more complicated by the number of right-angled joints. The plant stand incorporates a shallow tray at the top and a shelf at the bottom to hold a collection of plant pots. It is intended for both outdoor and indoor use. The gridded design has been painted a pale "bone" color, but other neutral shades would be equally effective.

The idea of grouping elements together to increase their impact is as important in garden design as it is in the design of interiors. Filled with geraniums, the plant stand would brighten up a corner of a patio or seating area, while, positioned near the kitchen door, either outside or in, the stand would also make a convenient home for a collection of herbs grown in containers.

PLANT STAND

This simple stand for plants and flowers looks equally good in the garden or the conservatory. The plant stand shown here is made from S4S (smooth 4 sides) softwood and then painted. However, if you want to retain the natural wood finish, then be sure to make it from good-quality softwood or even from hardwood, which can afterward be treated with a water-repellent preservative stain.

The design of the frame uses a number of wood joints, and for ease of assembly we suggest that these are doweled together. For a stronger job, the joints could be mortised and tenoned, but unless you have a mortising machine it would be too time-consuming (and complicated) to attempt to construct the frame by this method.

TOOLS

WORKBENCH (fixed or portable)

UTILITY KNIFE

STEEL MEASURING TAPE

STEEL BENCH RULE

TRY SQUARE

SMALL CROSSCUT SAW (or circular power saw)

BACK SAW (or power saber saw)

CHISEL

MARKING GAUGE

POWER DRILL

TWIST DRILL BIT – $\frac{1}{8}$in (3mm)

DOWELING JIG

BRAD-POINT BIT – $\frac{3}{8}$in (10mm)

MALLET

SCREWDRIVER

POWER SANDER (or hand sanding block)

MATERIALS

Part	Quantity	Material	Length
CORNER POSTS	4	2 × 2in (50 × 50mm) S4S softwood	30$\frac{5}{8}$in (779mm)
MIDDLE POSTS	2	As above	28in (711mm)
LONG RAILS	6	As above	33$\frac{3}{8}$in (847mm)
END RAILS	6	As above	9$\frac{5}{16}$in (237mm)
VERTICAL PIECES	10	As above	4$\frac{3}{4}$in (122mm)
SHELVES	2	$\frac{1}{4}$in (6mm) plywood	10$\frac{5}{8}$ × 34$\frac{5}{8}$in (270 × 880mm)
FEET	4	Offcut of hardwood or softwood	3$\frac{1}{2}$ × 3$\frac{1}{2}$ × 1$\frac{1}{8}$in (90 × 90 × 30mm)

Also required: $\frac{3}{8}$in (10mm) diameter doweling; 2in (50mm) No. 8 galvanized screws; brads

FRAME CONSTRUCTION

Cut all the components to length, following the Materials chart.

MAKING THE END FRAMES

Cut a half-lap joint to form the intersection of the middle post with the middle end rail (see **Techniques, page 152**). Mark off on the middle post where the middle end rail will cross it using one of the short vertical pieces as a spacer. The top of the cross half-lap joint will be this distance down from the top of the middle post.

Carefully mark out and cut the half-lap joint on the middle post and the middle end rail (fig. 1). Repeat for the other end frame.

Strike diagonal lines to mark the center points for the dowel holes on the ends of all the end rails, on the ends of the middle posts, and on the ends of all the short vertical pieces. Using a doweling jig and a dowel bit (or a drill fitted with a brad-point bit and held in a vertical drill stand) drill $\frac{3}{8}$in (10mm) diameter holes centrally into the marked positions. The hole depths should be slightly over half the dowel lengths (ie, $\frac{7}{8}$in [22mm] deep holes for 1$\frac{1}{2}$in [40mm] long dowels). This gives a small cavity at the end which will accommodate trapped air and glue (see **Techniques, Dowel joint, page 154**).

1 **Affixing Middle End Rail**
Mark position of middle end rail on middle post and cut half-lap joints to affix the two pieces together.

2 **Top and Bottom End Rails**
Mark dowel hole positions centrally on both ends of middle rail. Dowel to top and bottom end rails to affix.

3 **Adding Corner Posts**
Dowel posts to end rails: top end rail is flush with top of posts, bottom end rail flush with bottom of posts.

PLANT STAND ASSEMBLY

TOP LONG RAIL

TOP END RAIL

MIDDLE LONG RAIL

MIDDLE END RAIL

CORNER POST

MIDDLE POST

DOWELS

BOTTOM END RAIL

END FRAME

SMALL VERTICAL PIECES

LADDER SECTION

TOP SHELF

BOTTOM LONG RAIL

BOTTOM SHELF

PLANT STAND

Mark out the position of the top and bottom end rails onto the inside faces of the corner posts and strike diagonals again to mark the positions of the dowel holes. Drill the holes as before. Also mark out on each corner post the dowel hole positions for the middle rail, which is the same distance down as the length of a short vertical piece plus the $1\frac{1}{2}$in (38mm) depth of the top end rail. Square around onto the other internal face of each corner post to mark the dowel hole positions to take the top, middle, and bottom long rails.

Dry assemble the middle post and the middle end rail together to form a cross, and then dowel on the top and bottom end rails, again without glue (fig. 2, page 90). Complete the dry assembly of the end frames by adding the corner posts (fig. 3, page 90).

FRONT AND BACK FRAMES

To make up the front and back frames, which look like ladders, mark the positions of the short vertical pieces along one long rail, and mark dowel hole centers regularly and centrally along the rail (fig. 1). There is an internal spacing of $4\frac{1}{2}$in (110mm) between each short vertical piece, and also between the end-most vertical pieces and each of the corner posts.

Use this rail as a pattern to transfer the marks onto three of the other long rails. Drill all the dowel holes to the required depth and dry assemble the ladder frame sections.

Drill the dowel holes on the inside of the corner posts, using the marks transferred from the front and back ladder frame construction.

Mark the dowel hole positions centrally on the ends of the bottom long rails, then drill the holes in them and in the bottoms of the corner posts as before.

Dowel and dry assemble each ladder frame section, together with the long bottom rails, into the corner posts of the end frames (fig. 2).

Make sure that the assembly is square and fits together perfectly, dismantle in reverse order, then re-assemble, this time gluing the joints using waterproof wood adhesive.

SHELVES

The two shelves are cut so that they finish half-way across the thickness of the frame, rather than fitting flush with the outside edges of the frame rails. Notch out the corners and the central part at the ends to fit around the middle and corner posts.

Cut out the bottom shelf to fit onto the bottom rails, and glue and nail it down to the frame (fig. 3).

The top shelf is glued and nailed to the underside of the middle rails.

FEET

The feet are fitted underneath each corner and protrude at the sides and ends by the same amount as the "step" for the bottom shelf (that is, approximately $\frac{3}{4}$in [19mm]) (fig. 4). Any offcut of softwood or hardwood can be used to make them.

Apply waterproof wood adhesive, then screw the feet to the rails using two screws for each foot.

Fill any gaps using an exterior-grade wood filler. Finally, paint as required or apply a water-repellent wood preservative stain.

1 **Adding Vertical Pieces**
Vertical pieces are doweled in place at equal internal spacings between top and middle long rails.

2 **Frame Assembly**
Mark dowel positions on corner posts and ends of top, middle, and bottom long rails. Drill and join.

3 **Adding Bottom Shelf**
Cut shelf to finish half-way across frame rails. Notch ends to fit around posts. Glue and screw in place.

4 **Adding the Feet**
Cut feet from offcuts of wood. Glue and screw them up into rails so that they protrude by about $\frac{3}{4}$in (19mm).

PONDS

An ornamental fish pond will enhance even the smallest garden, providing interest and pleasure with water lilies, reeds, and fish mingling with dragonflies, water beetles, and small frogs. Ponds are easy to install and require little maintenance.

There are various ways to build a pond, but to ensure success, the whole project needs to be carefully planned in advance, taking into account the way in which the pond will be constructed, its size, shape, and location.

First, consider shape and location. The former is purely a matter of taste – a question of whether you want a formal rectangle or would prefer a more natural, curved outline. The main consideration is how you see the whole design blending with your garden, although you should avoid an over-complicated design as this will make the pond more difficult and more expensive to build. The location of the pond is critical, however. Ideally, it should receive sunlight for at least half the day to enable flowering pond plants to thrive. You should try to keep it away from overhanging trees since the shade will not be good for plants and mosquitoes will be encouraged. Deciduous trees pose a particular problem in the fall, when leaves falling into the water can have a harmful effect on pond life if they are left to rot.

A pond at the end of a long garden may sound appealing, but remember that if you want to include a waterfall, underwater lights, or a fountain, you face the problem of running an electricity supply a considerable distance. Also, you may not be able to enjoy the sight of the pond from indoors.

The basic factors governing the size are the proportions of the garden and how much time and money you want to spend on the pond. You must ensure that the pond is not "lost" in the garden, nor must it completely dominate it. Do not make a pond too small since a "puddle" will not provide the right conditions for water, plants, and fish to harmonize. The minimum surface area is really about 38 square feet (3.5 square meters). A smaller pond will not allow the water to be aerated and so it may become cloudy, in which case you would need to install a filtration system.

Water depth should not create major problems. The main hazard is with water that is too shallow, causing the pond to overheat in hot weather (leaving the fish short of oxygen) and to freeze in winter. Anything between 16–30in (400–750mm) will enable an excellent selection of plants to flourish. You should include a 9in- (225mm-) wide planting shelf, about 9in (225mm) below the water surface. The shelf should run around most, if not all, of the perimeter of the pond.

POND TYPES

Although a pond can be built using concrete to form the walls and base, few people would attempt this method nowadays since construction can be both tedious and difficult, and the pond may be prone to leaking and cracking. The two most common methods today involve using a preformed pond or a liner.

With a preformed pond, the size and shape of the pond is governed by the models available, whereas a liner allows you to create whatever shape you want. If you decide on a special shape or a very large pond, then you will have to use a liner, but otherwise both types have advantages and disadvantages when it comes to installation.

The choice of material to line a pond is between synthetic rubber and PVC. Although any type of liner can be pierced by sharp objects such as stones or digging implements being thrust into the water, this is less likely to happen with the thicker, better-quality types. Even an economy-grade liner can

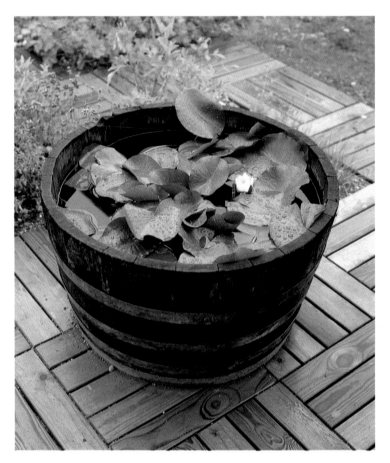

A POND FOR A PATIO

Not all gardens will have space for a full-size pond. A half-barrel provides a simple solution that is easy to maintain and will have space for two or three small goldfish and for colorful water lilies.

be expected to last ten years if it is properly installed and respected.

Colors readily available are black, stone, blue or gray. Although stone, blue and gray are more natural, many people prefer black since it is much less obtrusive in use. However, color is not vitally important since, after a while, the base of the pond will be covered with a thin layer of mud and its sides will be coated with algae.

A liner can be used in an above ground pond where the walls are constructed from brick or ornamental stonework. It can also be set into the ground in a level excavation made to the required depth and shape. In this case, sharp objects must be removed from the excavation and a 1in (25mm) layer of sand spread across the bottom. The liner is then placed in the excavation, the edges weighted with bricks, and water then added. The pressure of the water stretches the liner to the shape of the excavation.

Finally, paving slabs are used to make a border around the pond and to conceal the edge of the liner.

Preformed ponds are made from plastic or (more expensively) fiber-glass and can also be used above or below ground. In both cases, it is vital to support the sides and to ensure that the rim is exactly level.

The lesser-quality plastic ponds are neither as big nor as strong, but should certainly last for at least ten years and enable you to enjoy a wildlife pond in that time. However, if you really want a stock of outstanding fish and plants then you will need one of the better-quality models, which will last for years if it is properly installed and not damaged by sharp objects.

Whether you plan the pond to be below or above ground, it is vital that the excavation of the framework of bricks or ornamental stonework is lined with sand to provide adequate support for every nook and cranny of the pond's outline as the water exerts pressure on it.

PLANTS

Choose a mixture of types for the best effect; most are grown in plastic containers resting on the base of the pond or on the shelf.

Water lilies are a must, really, while shallow water marginals can be either tall and spikey or ground-covering. Deep water aquatics have their roots in containers but their leaves float on the surface, giving interest and shade to the water. Floating plants do not need soil for their roots and some only rise to the surface when flowering. Oxygenating plants, as the name suggests, supply oxygen to the pond and discourage algae. Use four or five for every square yard (meter) of water surface.

Almost inevitably, weeds will build up in the pond. Pull up weeds regularly: if the size and location of the pond allow, simply reach into the water and weed by hand; otherwise, use a rake or a long stick for any parts of the pond that are inaccessible. On no account, however, should you use a chemical algicide. Not only will it kill off the weed, leaving it to decompose in the pond, it may also contaminate your plant and fish stock.

There are many kinds of fish you can use to stock the pond apart from the ubiquitous goldfish, so read a bit about the subject and visit a good local specialist shop or a garden center with a pond department to see what is available.

BARREL POND

Any watertight container can be used for a small water garden and a half-barrel is one of the most popular choices. Half-barrels that previously contained beer, wine, or vinegar are normally available from large garden centers.

It is important to scrub clean the inside of the barrel first using only clean water, never detergent. A clean barrel is important because otherwise the water will quickly become contaminated, posing a threat to your plants and fish. For this reason do not use a barrel that previously contained either wood preservative or oil.

When you are satisfied that the barrel is thoroughly clean, spread 3–4in (75–100mm) of clean soil in the base of the barrel – keep out weeds or vegetation which will rot and pollute the water. Add enough water to enable you to mix the soil into a slurry of mud.

Planting should be carried out in spring or early summer. Use minia-ture water lilies and some other small, less vigorous plants. Include oxygenating plants to help keep the water clear.

Next, spread a 2in (50mm) layer of fine gravel over the soil to prevent the fish stirring it up and to help prevent the plants from becoming uprooted. Then fill the barrel with water through a hose with its nozzle inside a polyethylene bag (fig. 2); this prevents the jet of water disturbing the soil.

When the barrel is almost full, turn off the water and remove the bag and hose. Allow about a week for the water to settle and the temperature to stabilize before introducing the fish – two or three small goldfish – and a few snails. The fish will discourage mosquitoes in summer, but do transfer them to a larger pond or to a fishtank indoors for the winter as the small amount of water in a barrel is almost certain to freeze over in a cold winter. In early spring, before returning the fish to the barrel, replace most or all of the water and allow it to settle and the temperature to stabilize as before.

❶ Through-section of Pond with Liner
A hole of the required dimensions is dug and lined with sand before the liner is laid in place. Include a planting shelf around the perimeter. The liner is held in place at the edges by bricks, stones, or paving slabs.

❷ Making a Pond from a Half-barrel
Scrub the barrel clean and place a layer of soil at the bottom for planting. A layer of fine gravel prevents soil mixing with water. Fill pond with water through a hose with its nozzle in a polyethylene bag.

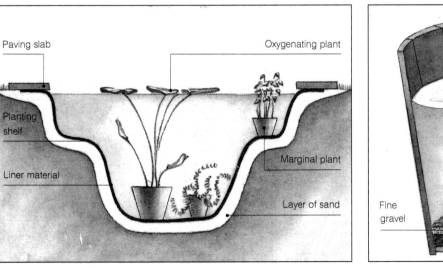

Paving slab
Oxygenating plant
Planting shelf
Liner material
Marginal plant
Layer of sand

Fine gravel
Hose
Polyethylene bag
Soil

PART 4

SUPPORTS AND DIVIDERS

The opposition of closed and open space is fundamental in garden design. All gardens have boundaries, more or less secure perimeters defined by walls, fences, or hedges. But often there is a need to break up space within the garden, dividing one part from another, screening the view of a utility area or vegetable garden, or making a garden "room," an enclosed area which can create a heightened sense of "hazard and surprise." Simple boundaries can be made from living dividers such as hedges, through semi-transparent picket, wattle, and beanstick fencing to proper garden walls of brick or stone.

Moving from a rose-covered pergola to an expanse of lawn is far more pleasing than walking along an exposed path. Framing a view with a simple arch, dissolving a boundary wall with climbers trained over a trellis, creating an arbor in a corner of the garden are all design devices which add depth and perspective to what might otherwise be flat and monotonous. By growing plants up pergolas, arbors, and other dividers you have the opportunity to add light and shade: the dappled sunlight created by foliage is one of the most appealing sights in the garden.

SUPPORTS AND DIVIDERS

Lattice is indispensable. Off-the-shelf square or diamond wooden mesh is available very cheaply, ready treated, in panels which can be assembled to create a variety of structures or to cover a large surface area. As an extension to a boundary fence, trellis covered with climbing plants filters the wind so that it cannot cut across the garden, and gives a degree of privacy without entirely blocking airflow and light. It is also one of the most economical ways of getting rid of eyesores – ugly sheds, bare blank walls in stock brick, concrete blocks, anything which cannot easily be removed can be covered with trellis and plants encouraged to grow. Climbers such as Russian vine (*Fallopia aubertii*) and flowering plants such as clematis, climbing roses, honeysuckle (*Lonicera* sp) and Virginia creeper (*Parthenocissus quinquefolia*) can materially alter the appearance of any structure. Wisteria will need a greater degree of support, and ivy should be avoided at all costs: its aerial roots dig into mortar and damage brickwork. You can also use trellis to make free-standing structures to block unwelcome views.

Trellis can be put to more positive use, to create a whole range of effects. *Treillages*, intricate flat wooden frameworks, were a feature of French formal gardens, traditionally painted green and used against ecru walls. These were often arched, with tapering lines that gave a subtle sense of perspective – a simple *trompe l'oeil* that enlivened Parisian courtyards. Less elaborate trellis still has this ability to "dissolve" a flat, dull expanse of wall. Depending on how positive you want the trellis to be, you can stain or paint it to add interest in the winter when the leaves have fallen. Trellis helps to blend and merge the garden with the house, taking greenery up onto walls, the sides of buildings and fences.

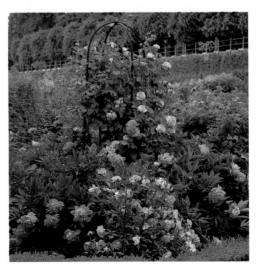

A pergola is another type of support for plants, but one which involves some kind of canopy, either as a free-standing arch, a covered walkway or a simple framework projecting out from the side of the house. It is commonplace in Mediterranean countries to attach a plain metal framework and wiring to the house over a rear courtyard or front entrance and allow a vine to create a type of living awning. The leaves of the vine keep the sun off and deflect the heat in the summer; in the winter, the frame and the house are revealed: a cheap, effective solution and one which generates interest by changing from month to month. Plain or painted trellis can also be used overhead; the grid takes the strength out of the sun and makes a lively pattern of light and shade.

In design terms, a pergola acts as a kind of picture frame, intensifying a view. It usually demands some type of focal point – a seat or urn at the end of a walkway, for example. But it also produces a contrast of light and shade which is so attractive in a garden, and it makes an ideal support for plants, since they are freely exposed to sunlight, air, and rain.

While there is something especially English about a rose-covered pergola, it is the French who excel at garden ironmongery, including that wonderful green iron which goes to make curved frameworks, such as the one which forms the laburnum avenue in Monet's garden at Giverny. There are different ways of making a pergola, but, generally, if you want the top to curve it must be made of metal, although it is possible to wire beanpoles to achieve a curve. A simple version is to attach small sections of curved metal to wooden uprights. Wires for training plants can be passed through holes in the metal frame or trellis attached to the posts to support climbing roses, honeysuckle, and espaliered and cordoned fruit trees.

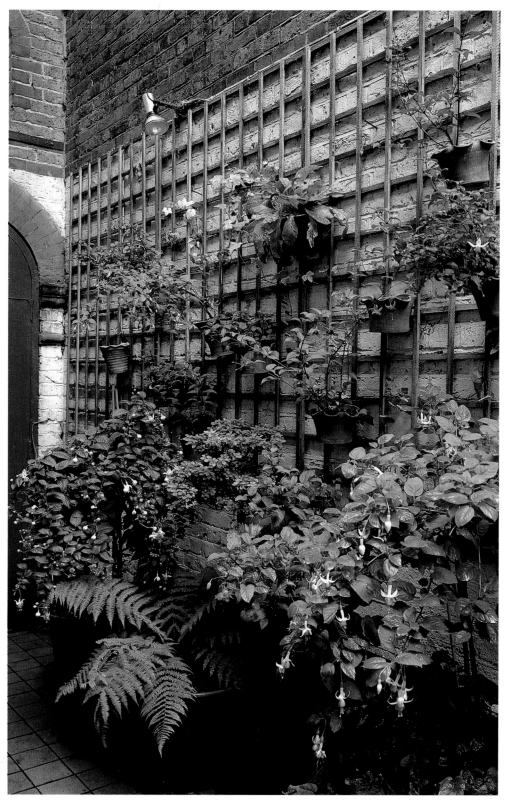

TRELLISWORK

Trellis is much more than just a support for plants. Trompe l'oeil *designs add wit and interest to plain expanses of wall (opposite above and opposite center). Trellis can also be attached to free-standing copper pipes or posts and used to support climbing roses and other plants (opposite below). For an urban garden, with little horizontal growing space, trellis provides a vertical extension, acting as a support for potted plants (left).*

ALL FENCED IN

Most people need some means to mark boundaries, either with a neighboring house or between different areas of the garden (overleaf). The style of fencing you choose should reflect and enhance the overall design of your garden: use white painted fencing to contrast with bright flowers, natural wood posts for a country feel, or strongly geometric panels for a look of urban chic.

Supports and Dividers

Another type of garden enclosure or room is the arbor. Essentially a seat shaded by a canopy of plants, the arbor always adds a certain mysterious, romantic quality to a garden. As well as its visual impact, there is often the added dimension of the perfume of scented flowers growing overhead. The framework itself can be as simple as you like. Trellis is a good component, but special metal arbor frameworks are also available.

There is great diversity in the materials and methods used to create boundaries in a garden. While there is no need to look for an exact match to the design of your house, some styles of fence and wall will be more appropriate than others. Metal railings, of the kind seen in public parks, are generally better in town situations; stockade fencing and split rail fencing are really for the country. Avoid, if you can,

building walls in cheap stock bricks which never weather; concrete blocks and concrete posts and wire mesh fencing can also be unappetizing. An existing wall which presents this kind of eyesore can be ameliorated either by covering it with trellis or, in the case of a concrete structure, encouraging the growth of lichens and moss.

Semi-transparent boundaries can be made cheaply with trellis, using standard panels secured to posts. Today you can buy spiked steel socket-type supports which make the job of sinking posts much easier. Inspiration for other types of wooden or panel fencing can be taken from the Japanese, who excel at Mondrian-type arrangements of panels and screens using bamboo uprights and woven rush, roughly equivalent to European traditional wattle fencing.

Wall building is an art in itself. There are many intriguing and inspiring examples: stone inset with flints, shells, pebbles, or bottle ends; dry stone walling; brick walls built with spaces to let air and views through; walls made of logs and driftwood. It is a good idea, if you are building a wall from scratch, to leave pockets so that plants can be grown on the vertical face. Alyssum, thrift, aubrieta, campanula, and other rock plants will grow in cornices, wall pockets and on tops of dry stone walling.

Hedges are the living boundaries in a garden, easy on the eye, good at creating windbreaks and relatively simple to maintain. As far as types are concerned, there are many alternatives to the ubiquitous privet. Box (although slow-growing), beech, yew, and hawthorn all make excellent and attractive hedges.

ARBORS

Structures which provide a support for climbing and trailing plants also make ideal locations for garden seats, creating a shady, scented retreat from which to view the garden. Aesthetically, an arbor also provides contrast of light and shade which is so important in giving depth and definition to a layout.

WALK-THROUGH PERGOLA

In a small garden, a pergola, or frame-work for climbing plants, makes an architectural addition which gives focus to the entire layout, especially when centrally positioned. In a larger garden, a pergola can be extended further to create a proper walkway, a semi-enclosed space to contrast with the open areas of lawn and flowerbed. This particular design can be adapted to vary the length as required, but would not really be effective if made any shorter than three units long.

The structure and the dimensions of the pergola are based around standard trellis panels, which are much cheaper than any you could make for the purpose.

The easiest way to assemble the structure is to construct the top frame first, adding the struts to make the pyramid roof afterwards. Then the position of the posts, or uprights, can be marked out on the ground where you want the pergola to go and metal shoes or spiked steel supports driven in.

The final stage is to cover the outside of the structure with trellis. When viewed from the side, the trellis wall appears to be continuous, but, because the trellis is affixed to alternate bays, you will get glimpses of the garden as you walk through. As a plain, undressed structure with no covering of plants the pergola has its own attractions, especially when painted a strong positive color. To support climbing plants over the roof, simply staple wire around the pyramids.

Walk-through Pergola

The light and airy framework of this pergola can be built over a garden path to form a covered walkway of colorful and sweet-scented climbing plants trained over the easy-to-make, but distinctive, trellis and wire-covered framework. Good plants to use include clematis, especially the small-flowered species such as *C. montana* and *C. armandii*, climbing hydrangea (*H. petiolaris*), sweet-scented plants such as jasmine and honeysuckle, and wisteria. The many varieties of ivy are quickly established, although they can be difficult to contain; instead, you could try ornamental grape vines, the leaves of which turn to spectacular colors in the fall.

The "roof" is a series of simple pyramids on a wooden framework which is affixed on top of fence posts held upright by hammer-in steel fence post supports. Training wires for climbing plants are stapled around the pyramids, and trellis panels are attached at the sides between the post supports.

Trellis panels (lattice) usually come in 72in (1830mm) widths, and in heights of 24in (600mm), 36in (900mm) and 48in (1220mm). For this project, the panels are turned to give a height of 72in (1830mm) and a width of 48in (1220mm).

The size of the trellis panels also determines the dimensions of the pergola – ours is 48in (1220mm) wide, and the posts are spaced 48in (1220mm) apart. It is best to keep these measurements the same so that the "base" to each pyramid is a square, ensuring that the struts are in proportion to the main frame. The height of the posts is 6ft 6in (2m) which means that the trellising is raised off the ground 6in (150mm). We have only fixed trellising to alternate bays, but this is simply for effect. Our pergola is four bays long, but this is variable and you can have more or fewer bays, according to your requirements.

All wood used is sawn and pre-servative-treated softwood, as used for fencing.

PYRAMID ROOF STRUCTURE

The series of pyramids that form the "roof" of the pergola add visual interest to the design. Training wires are stapled around the struts, enabling plants to grow and thrive and to form a "living ceiling."

MATERIALS

Note: All lumber is sawn and preservative-treated softwood

Part	Quantity	Material	Length
LONG RAILS	2	2 × 3in (50 × 75mm)	17ft 3in (5.25m)
CROSS RAILS	5	As above	48in (1200mm)
PYRAMID STRUTS	16	1 × 3in (25 × 75mm)	53in (1350mm)*
POSTS	10	3 × 3in (75 × 75mm)	6ft 6in (2m)
TRELLIS PANELS (LATTICE)	8		72in (1830mm) high × 48in (1200mm)
HAMMER-IN POST SUPPORTS	10		
TRAINING WIRE	1 large coil		
SCREWS		Galvanized steel	2in (50mm) No. 8
STAPLES		Galvanized fencing type	$\frac{3}{4}$in (19mm)

* Approximate length only – measure and cut on site for accuracy

TOOLS

WORKBENCH (fixed or portable)

STEEL MEASURING TAPE

STEEL BENCH RULE

TRY SQUARE

COMBINATION SQUARE

SMALL CROSSCUT SAW (or circular power saw)

BACK SAW

MARKING GAUGE

POWER DRILL

DRILL BIT – approximately $\frac{1}{8}$in (3mm) diameter to drill pilot holes for screws

SLEDGE HAMMER

CLAW HAMMER

CHISEL – about 1in (25mm)

MALLET

WALK-THROUGH PERGOLA ASSEMBLY

TRAINING WIRES

PYRAMID STRUT

CROSS RAIL

LONG RAIL

STEEL POST SUPPORT

POST

TRELLIS PANEL

WALK-THROUGH PERGOLA

TOP FRAME

Start by making the top frame on which the "roof" of pyramids is affixed and which will eventually be supported on the vertical posts. The top long rails are made from 2 × 3in (50 × 75mm) sawn and preservative-treated wood, ideally in one full length (that is, if you are making the pergola to the proportions shown in the photograph, the length of four trellis panels plus the five posts of nominal 3in [75mm] width). If it is impossible to buy wood the length required, two shorter lengths can be joined end to end with a simple cross-lap joint (see **Techniques, page 152**).

Cut the cross rails to the width required, in our case 53in (1345mm) (the spacing between two posts plus the thickness of the posts).

Mark out the positions of the posts on the long rails to suit the width of the trellis panels, in our case at *internal* intervals of 48in (1220mm). Cut cross-lap joints at the appropriate places on the long

rails and at the ends of the cross rails, so that they form end-lap joints on the cross rails at either end (fig. 1) and half-lap joints on the intermediate rails (see **Techniques, page 152**). Form the joints so that the long rails are on top.

Screw the joints together through the cross rails from the underside.

PYRAMID ROOF SECTIONS

To work out the exact length of the pyramid struts, measure the diagonal of the base across the frame. Mark this length on a flat floor and strike equal length lines at 45° to this line at either end to give the point of the apex of the pyramid. This gives the lengths of the timber required for the structure forming the pyramid – the measurement should more or less correspond to the length of the cross rails.

Cut the required number of struts slightly overlength and then miter them all at 45° at both ends in opposite directions and to the correct length required.

To assemble, hold two of the struts in a vise so the mitered faces of one end meet. Screw through each side using 2in (50mm) No. 8 galvanized woodscrews (fig. 2).

Hold this frame upright in a workbench and lay a third strut against the joint and pilot drill through at approximately 45° into the other frame (fig. 3). Repeat for the fourth pyramid strut (fig. 4).

Make up the required number of pyramid structures. These are delicate, so handle them carefully.

Place each pyramid on top of the frame already made and screw down into it with a single screw at each corner (fig. 5). Once secured, this is a very strong structure. Repeat for all of the pyramids.

Staple training wires at 6in (150mm) intervals up the pyramids.

AFFIXING THE POSTS AND FINAL ASSEMBLY

Carry the top structure to its final position and use it to mark on the ground the positions of the fence posts. The posts are spaced at

internal intervals of 48in (1220mm) so that they coincide with the cross rail positions.

The easiest way to secure the posts is with steel post supports. These are simply hammered into the ground and the posts slotted into sockets at the tops of the supports.

Stretch a string line along the line of the posts. This string line will help you to line up the supports and will also give some idea of levels. Push the tip of the support into the ground and use a carpenter's level to check that it is upright. To drive the support into the ground, a heavy hammer, such as a sledge hammer, will be required. Insert a short length of 3 × 3in (75 × 75mm) wood post into the socket to protect the support from hammer blows, or use a proprietary metal-capped driving tool which should have a handle allowing you to steady the socket and prevent it from twisting as it is hammered in place.

Drive the support into the ground with firm, slow blows of the hammer. At regular intervals, insert a post into the socket and use a carpenter's

① Joining Top Frame Rails
Frame rails form end lap joints at ends and half lap joints (not shown) at intermediate points.

② Joining First Two Struts
Miter ends of struts at 45° and butt cut faces together. *Inset* Affix with screws at oblique angles.

③ Adding Remaining Struts
Hold frame in a workbench. Screw through from sides of third strut to face of joint; repeat for fourth strut.

④ Apex of Finished Pyramid
Finished joints form pyramid apex. *Inset* Angled screws attach third and fourth struts to first two struts.

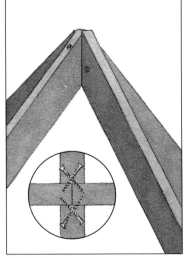

level on two adjacent faces to check that the spike is going in vertically. Adjustments can be made by pulling or twisting the sockets as necessary.

When the supports have been inserted the posts can be fitted. In some designs of post supports, two bolts have to be tightened to clamp the posts in position, while in others the posts are held with large screws. Double-check that the posts are upright and use a length of straight lumber and a carpenter's level to check that the tops of the posts are level. On flat or slightly sloping ground this will be easy to achieve, but on steeply sloping ground it may be acceptable if the tops of the posts follow the slope of the ground. Use a length of string or a long batten to level the post tops which can be trimmed to an even height, if necessary, using a crosscut saw.

The next stage is to install the trellising between the posts (we installed it only to alternate bays of the pergola). Place bricks or blocks on the ground to support the trellis panels about 6in (150mm) from the ground. We used metal clips to hold

the panels of trellis in place and the clips are first nailed to the posts so that they are vertical and inset by the same amount – about 1in (25mm). The panels are then lifted into place and a check is made that the horizontal rails of the trellis panels are level. The panels are then secured to the clips using galvanized screws *(see* **Techniques, page 152** *)*.

If required, the trellis panels can be secured directly to the posts. Position and level them as above, then drill through the side frames of the panels so that 3in (75mm) long galvanized fencing nails can be driven through the panels, without splitting them, and into the posts. Three fixings will be required on each side of a 72in (1830mm) high trellis panel.

You will need some help to lift the pyramid roof onto the posts. Adjust the roof so that the vertical posts coincide with the corner and cross rail joints, then nail the frame to the tops of the posts using two 4in (100mm) nails toe-nailed through the top frame and into each post.

5 **Affixing Pyramids to Frame**
Screw the pyramids to the top frame using a screw through each corner and into the frame rails.

TRELLIS WITH FALSE PERSPECTIVE

Trellising has varied garden applications. This project goes a stage further and follows the French tradition of using trellis to give blank walls a sense of depth and perspective. The result, although simple to construct, is a memorable and effective exercise in *trompe-l'oeil*. You can adapt this idea to cheer up any featureless expanse of wall or disguise unsympathetic stock brick or concrete block.

Perhaps the easiest project in the book to accomplish, this false-perspective trellis could be assembled without too much trouble during the course of a single afternoon once you have established your required dimensions and perspective.

The first step is to draw up a full-size plan: you can adapt the design shown here to fit your space. A false perspective is generally more effective if you arrange it so there is a contrast with a real view. Incorporating a doorway, as here, or any other kind of opening heightens the element of "hazard and surprise."

The next stage is to nail together slats of wood to make the required design. Bend the nails over and hammer them flat as they go through the back so they will not pull out. If you want a curved arch, you could make the curve out of exterior-grade plywood cut with a saber saw.

This trellis design was painted a pale gray to blend with the lichened wall. Trellis looks very effective painted, but the colors should not be too harsh and bright or the illusory effect will be lost.

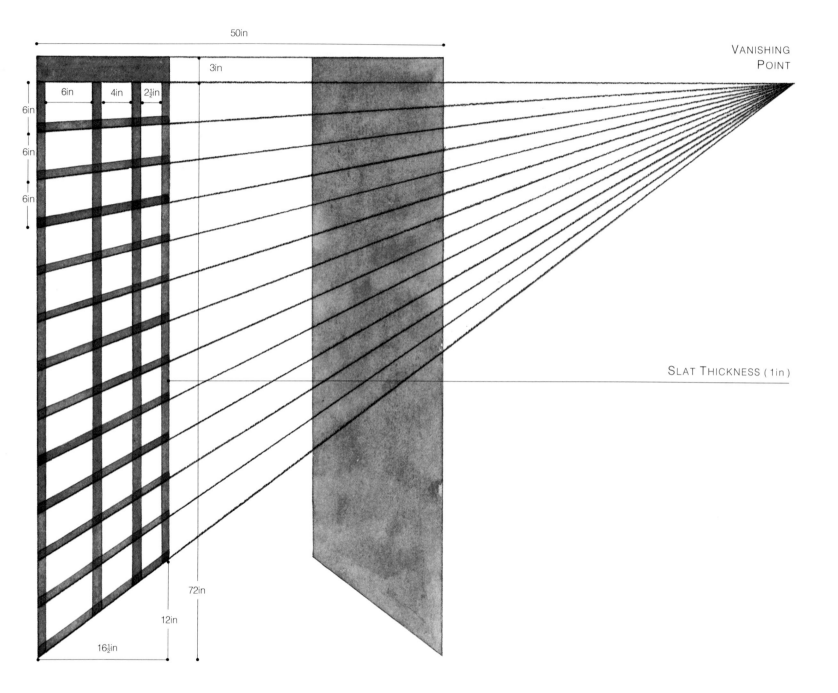

VANISHING POINT

50in

3in

6in | 4in | 2½in

6in

6in

6in

SLAT THICKNESS (1in)

72in

12in

16½in

DRAWING UP A PLAN OF THE TRELLIS STRUCTURE

You will need to draw up a full-size plan to calculate the length of the slats and the degree of perspective. The overall height and width shown here are based on the dimensions of the door alongside which we built this project, and can be altered according to the space available.

TRELLIS WITH FALSE PERSPECTIVE

This trellis is constructed so that when it is fixed against a wall, it deceives the eye into believing it is looking at a three-dimensional arch, or a series of three-dimensional arches if several are installed side by side as shown here.

If you fit the trellis around a door or gateway, sizes are dependent on the dimensions of the door. We used three archways alongside a garden door, which has a matching trellis "roof" above it. Our arches are separated by 1 × 3in (25 × 75mm) wooden "posts" beveled at the top. However, the principles of construction are easy to adapt to other sizes and designs according to the size of your garden, the amount of wall space, and personal preference.

A wider batten has also been incorporated at the top to align with the top of the door frame, replacing one of the "normal size" trellis slats, but again this is optional.

The density of the trellis and the amount of perspective incorporated is entirely up to individual taste, but the dimensions here are a good standard to work from.

Obviously, you will need a wall on which to affix the trellis. This need not be a garden boundary wall: it could be a plain wall of the house, or the wall of a garage or outbuilding.

1 **Drawing Up a Plan of the Roof Structure**
Above Draw a line to trellis width. Draw a line perpendicular to center point – top of this line represents apex. Draw in slat thickness, then two sides of triangle. Mark where vertical slats of side panels fall along base and extend lines to center line, parallel with triangle sides. Mark five equally spaced points on each side and join to center of base.

TOOLS

WORKBENCH (fixed or portable)

STEEL MEASURING TAPE

TRY SQUARE

BACK SAW (or saber saw)

CLAW HAMMER

POWER DRILL

DRILL BIT – $\frac{3}{16}$in (4mm)

MASONRY DRILL BIT – $\frac{1}{4}$in (6mm)

SCREWDRIVER

CARPENTER'S LEVEL

MATERIALS

Note: If you experience difficulty buying $\frac{1}{2}$ × 1in (12 × 25mm), you can cut your own slats by ripping down 1 × 8in (25 × 200mm) wood using a circular saw; this will give 16 slats per board if saw blade is not too thick

Part	Quantity	Material	Length
VERTICAL SLATS	8 per trellis arch	$\frac{1}{2}$ × 1in (12 × 25mm) sawn softwood	72in (1800mm)*
CROSS SLATS	As required	As above	As required
ROOF SLATS	As required	As above	As required
TOP BATTEN (optional)	1 per arch	$\frac{1}{2}$ × 3in (12 × 75mm) sawn softwood	50in (1270mm)**
POST	1 between each arch	1 × 3in (25 × 75mm) sawn softwood	As required

* Finished size – cut overlong and then cut to size after nailing (see text for details)

** Length given is width of each trellis arch; top battens can be cut from two shorter lengths of softwood because center section is cut away on assembly

CONSTRUCTION

The easiest way to make this trellis is first to draw up full-size plans on a large, reasonably flat surface such as a garage floor, tables pushed together, or a flat area of concrete, such as a driveway.

You may be able to draw the plan directly onto your flat surface, but it is more likely that you will have to make the drawing on several sheets of paper which can then be taped together to produce a full-size plan. Wherever you construct the trellis, it will be necessary to have enough space for all the pieces to be laid out on this plan and nailed up in place on top of the drawing.

DRAWING UP PLANS

Using our diagrams as a guide, draw up plans for one side of the upright trellis. You need to decide on the height and spaces required. Ours is 72in (1800mm) high, with 12 equal spaces down the outer side, giving 6in (150mm) centers (actually from the base of one slat to the base of the next).

Mark off the width of this one side of trellis; ours is 16¼in (410mm) from the outside edge of the outermost vertical slat to the inside edge of the innermost vertical slat. Two more vertical slats are placed between them to give *internal* spacings of 6in (150mm), 4in (100mm), and 2½in (60mm) respectively.

The innermost vertical slat is only 60in (1500mm) long and is placed 12in (300mm) up from the ground. Join the bottom two points and continue this angled line up until it meets a horizontal line drawn across at the very top. This gives you a vanishing point where the two lines cross. All the other cross lines must converge at this point.

Use a slat to mark off the thickness of all the slats across the width and down the length of the trellis.

Draw up the "roof" section next,

starting with the base line of the triangle. Find the center and draw a vertical line (at exactly 90°) up, 24in (600mm) long, to give the apex of the triangle. Draw in the slat thickness over this center line. Then draw in the outer lines of the triangle.

If you have made this drawing separate from the main trellis, mark off where the vertical slats of the main trellis will fall along the base line. Draw lines from these positions onto the roof section, parallel with the outer lines of the triangle, joining them all at the center line.

Equally space five points along each of the upward-sloping sides of the triangle (giving six equal spaces on each side) and join these points to the center of the base line. Start with the central one, and then space two slats on either side.

Draw in the other slat thicknesses as before, finishing the cross slats at the innermost roof slat (fig. 1).

Use the drawings to measure off for the lengths of slats that will be required (remembering to multiply the number of slats in the vertical structure by two), and then multiply the total by the number of arches required. Add on a little extra to each length to allow for trimming the angles at the ends.

When the slats have been obtained, cut them all to length, again allowing a small surplus to allow for trimming at the ends.

MAKING UP ONE SIDE

Start by laying all the cross slats accurately on the drawing, and then place the vertical slats on top.

Apply a dab of waterproof wood glue at every intersection of the slats, then affix by driving an annular threaded nail through each intersection. If you are nailing up on a workbench, a good way to hold the slats firm while nailing is to drive nails temporarily into the bench at all corners, where the slats cross each other. Make up the required number of trellis frames.

MAKING UP OPPOSITE SIDE

Turn over the first side of trellis panel, then draw around it onto the worksurface to give a mirror image of the plan. Make up the required number of trellis frames to this pattern in the same way as before.

MAKING UP THE ROOF

The roof is made in the same way as the side panels. Position the cross slats on the plan, and then place the long parallel slats on top. Glue and nail the intersections.

FINISHING OFF

Saw the protruding ends of the slats flush with the edges of the frames.

Prepare the "posts" and the top battens. In the latter case, the center section will be cut out on assembly, so you could use two offcuts for these pieces, rather than a batten the full width of the trellis arch.

Ideally, you should use preservative-treated timber. If not, at this stage treat the whole trellis with a water-repellent preservative. The finished trellis is painted with three coats of microporous paint, or one coat of exterior primer and two coats of exterior gloss paint.

AFFIXING THE TRELLIS

If the trellis is going to support climbing plants, spacers must be inserted between it and the wall so that plants can twine behind the trellis. Otherwise, the trellis can be screwed directly to the wall.

Position a post against the wall, and use a carpenter's level to check it is vertical. Drill clearance holes for two screws through the post and allow the drill tip to mark the wall. Remove the post and, using a masonry bit, drill the holes for the anchors. Insert the anchors, then drive galvanized screws through the post and into the plugs. The screws should penetrate the wall by about 1½in (38mm).

Affix the adjacent side panel and, using an offcut of top batten as a spacer, fit the roof section, then the next post, then the next roof trellis, then the next post, and so on right across. After this, add the other side trellises, with lengths of top batten, if required, attached between the top of the side panels and the undersides of the roof panels.

❷ Nailing the Trellis
Lay cross slats on plan, then position vertical slats above them. Glue and nail through intersections.

Hexagonal Arbor

An arbor makes a distinctive feature in any garden, displaying climbing plants to great advantage and exposing them to optimum conditions of light and air. Arbors are often all-metal structures, but this simple but elegant framework makes use of ordinary copper tubing and plain wooden rustic posts, readily available from most garden centers. The construction process is fairly quick and easy to do.

The three sections of copper tubing (which have been rubbed with plumbers' flux to give them a green color) are cut to precisely the same length and bent into shape using a curved piece of plywood or particleboard as a form. Holes are drilled about 6in (150mm) apart along the tubes. Thin green plastic-covered wires are threaded through the holes to make a support for the plants.

As is the case with all posts that need to go into the ground, it is much easier to use spiked steel supports with sockets. The metal spikes are readily driven into the ground and the end of the post can be dropped into the shoe and held in place.

The uprights and cross rails must be treated with a preservative and the resulting dark brown makes a pleasing contrast with the greenish copper.

HEXAGONAL ARBOR

This arbor is made from six preservative-treated rustic poles set into the ground at equal intervals and joined by cross rails, with a dome above made from copper tubing. If you brush the tubing with plumbers' flux, a green patina will result. Garden wire is fed around the tubing as a support for climbing plants.

WOODEN FRAME

The height of the frame can be varied slightly. However, the poles should not be less than about 6ft 6in (2m) above ground, otherwise some people may hit their heads on the cross rails; and, for stability, the poles should not be much higher above ground than 8ft (2.5m).

PREPARING THE SITE

Choose a flat site and, using pegs and string lines, mark out the hexagonal shape (fig. 1) for the positions. The posts are spaced at 39in (1000mm) centers, with 6ft 6in (2m) between any two opposite posts. It is essential that the post positions are accurately marked.

Dig 24in (600mm) deep holes for the posts. This can be done using a narrow spade or, if available, a post-hole digger which is driven into the ground and then removed to deposit excavated earth. Fill the bottom 6in (150mm) of each hole with gravel to ensure good drainage and prevent the bottoms of the posts from rotting.

MAKING THE FRAME

Make up six L-shapes comprising a post and a cross rail as follows.

Position two posts in neighboring holes and wedge them vertically. Measure the internal distance between them and add 2in (50mm) to allow for shaping the ends of the cross rails. Remove the posts.

Use a saber saw to make a curved cut in the ends of the cross rails so that they fit against the post sides. Alternatively, use a hand saw to cut out V-shapes in the cross rails.

At the top of each post, draw 60° angles as a guide to aligning the cross rails (fig. 2, below). Continue the lines to the opposite sides of the post as a guide for the dowel affixing positions. Cut the doweling into 6in (150mm) lengths.

Lay one post on a flat piece of ground. Position a cross rail against the post and drill through the post and into the rail to accept the dowel (fig. 3). At least 2in (50mm) of dowel should enter the rail. Fit the dowel using waterproof wood adhesive. Repeat to make five more L-shapes.

ERECTING THE FRAME

Position two posts in their holes and align the cross rail that falls between them with both posts. Use a straight edge and a carpenter's level to align the posts – if necessary, add or take away a little of the gravel in the base of the hole. Drill through the "free" post into the end of the cross rail to align with the angles marked on the top. Join the "free" post to the cross rail with a length of dowel as you did before (fig. 3).

Continue to join up the L-shaped sections in the same way, checking that the tops of the posts are all at the same height, and then saw off any protruding dowel ends flush with the posts.

MATERIALS

Part	Quantity	Material	Length
POSTS	6	3–4in (75–100mm) diameter treated rustic poles	7ft 8in (2.4m)
CROSS RAILS	6	2–3in (50–75mm) diameter treated rustic poles	As required
DOME BARS	3	$\frac{7}{8}$in (22mm) diameter copper tubing	As required

Also required: Approximately 6ft 6in (2m) of $\frac{1}{2}$in (12mm) diameter hardwood doweling

TOOLS

WORKBENCH (fixed or portable)

SPADE or POST-HOLE DIGGER

PANEL SAW

CARPENTER'S LEVEL

STEEL BENCH RULE

SABER SAW

POWER DRILL

HAMMER

SCREWDRIVER

PLIERS

HACKSAW

CLAMPS

SHOVEL

1 Drawing up a Ground Plan
Posts are spaced 39in (1000mm) apart: mark center and strike off 39in (1000mm) lines at 60° angles.

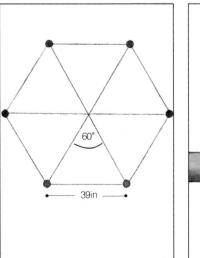

2 Shaping the Cross Rails
Angle ends of rails to fit around posts. Use saber saw for curve or make V-cuts with crosscut saw.

3 Affixing the Cross Rails
Drill holes through posts into cross rails. Insert dowels to affix in place. Angled screw holds dowel in place.

To secure the joints, use a 3in (75mm) screw inserted diagonally through each cross rail (fig. 3).

Finally, tie a length of garden wire around the top of the posts, holding it in place on each post using 1½in (38mm) staples. To make the wire taut, twist the two ends together using pliers.

THE DOME

Draw a semi-circle on a large sheet of plywood or particleboard (fig. 4) using a pencil and a piece of string to act as a compass. This will mark out the section of the dome. When this is done, mark off at 6in (150mm) centers for the positions of holes through which training wires will later be threaded.

Use a piece of ¾in (19mm) particleboard or plywood to make a form for bending the tube into shape. Trace the curve onto the form and cut it out using a saber saw.

BENDING THE TUBE

Cut the copper tubing to length using a hacksaw. Our tubes were 10ft 4in (3.14m) long. Since the copper will need to be bent a little tighter than the arc, bring it down about 1½in (38mm) at each end.

Clamp the form to a workbench or table and start to bend the piece of tube around it. You will need someone to help you with this: each person should exert a little pressure until the tubing is bent to follow the shape of the form. If you find that the ends lose their shape then you can use a ⅞in (22mm) internal pipe bending spring.

Lay the bent tube on the original dome profile and mark off the 6in (150mm) spacings onto the tube. Drill ⅛in (3mm) diameter holes through the tubing at these marks.

Bend the other two tubes to the shape of the form and then drill the holes as before. Always mark off the spacings on the tubing against the original dome profile.

ASSEMBLING THE DOME

Mark the middle point of each tube, then hammer it flat so that you can drill a ¼in (6mm) diameter hole through each piece (fig. 5). Bolt the three pieces together.

Next, drill a 1in (25mm) diameter hole, 2in (50mm) deep in the center of the top of each post.

The dome can now be lifted onto the top of the posts and the tube ends located in the holes (fig. 6). There is sufficient movement in the structure to enable the dome to be positioned.

Thread garden wire through each row of holes, tying each length securely in place.

To affix the dome to the rustic poles, drill straight through the tube horizontally above each post and slip a 2in (50mm) nail through.

Finally make up a dryish concrete mix of five parts sand to one part cement and pour it into each hole along with some small pieces of stone. Tamp it down, then shape it into a concave collar so that rain water will drain away.

4 Dome Section and Form
Mark off 6in (150mm) spacings on semi-circle. Transfer section of curve to plywood to make form.

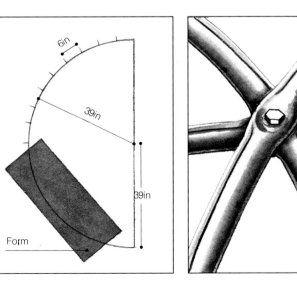

5 Affixing the Dome
Flatten out tops of the pieces of tubing, drill a ¼in (6mm) diameter hole through them and bolt together.

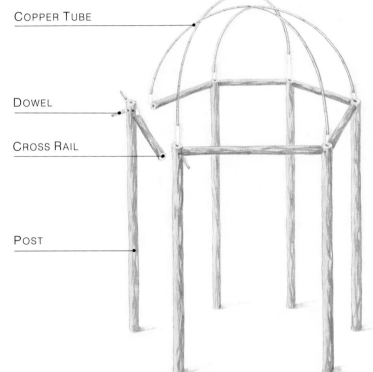

HEXAGONAL ARBOR ASSEMBLY

COPPER TUBE

DOWEL

CROSS RAIL

POST

6 Affixing Dome to Posts
Drill a hole centrally in the top of each post. Slot dome into post and drive nail through tubing.

BEANSTICK FENCE

New fencing can look rather harsh and brash and hedges, even when composed of the most quick-growing species, are unfortunately not instant solutions to the problem of garden enclosure. This beanstick fence was designed to provide a more natural-looking boundary than the standard commercial wood fencing; almost, in fact, a "man-made hedge." The look is reminiscent of the traditional wattle fence; another source of inspiration was the type of wonderful screens and panels seen in Japanese gardens and walkways. Here the effect is created by combining a strong rectilinear framework with the natural, random texture supplied by the beansticks.

The fence is very easy to make. The beansticks are trapped in the sawn frame, held in place in two grooves made top and bottom between the top rails and a couple of battens between the bottom rails. The sticks are cut to the same length, slotted into the groove and pushed up together.

The sticks themselves do not need to be treated, although the ends could be dipped in preservative to prolong their life. If sticks do become broken or damaged, it is easy to replace them.

This fence, formal enough for a front yard, would also be a good choice for a new house where the planting had not yet had a chance to become established. The beansticks are sufficiently firm and resilient to be animal-proof but chinks of light lend it a lively and varied effect.

BEANSTICK FENCE

This rustic-looking fence is an ideal project if you want your boundary to look just a bit different from those of your neighbors. It is made from beansticks secured between a frame of sawn and preservative-treated wood. This can be left in its natural state, it can be stained a darker wood color, or it can be painted as shown in our example – microporous paint is ideal for covering the wood, being easy to apply without a primer, and easy to repaint in future as the need arises.

It is unlikely that you will be able to buy the beansticks from a lumberyard. More likely sources are either from fencing suppliers or from garden centers.

Cutting of the beansticks is done in winter and early spring, and this is the best time to obtain the sticks. You will need large numbers for this project, and it is a good idea to buy one or two bundles of sticks to start with to see what proportion of the fence they cover. Then you will be able to put in an order for a quantity to cover the full length of the fence you will be making.

The spacing of the posts depends on the length of the rails you will be using. Rails must be joined at post positions, so if you have 10ft (3m) rails, posts must be spaced 60in (1500mm) apart. For 8ft (2.4m) rails, the post spacing will be 48in (1200mm). Once this is decided, you will be able to work out how many posts are required.

You also need to decide on the height of the posts. Our fence is about 40in (1000mm) high, and in this case the posts are 60in (1500mm) long which allows 20in (500mm) of post to be in the ground. A good rule is to allow a minimum of 20in (500mm) of post in the ground, or one third of the fence height, whichever is greater.

Alternatively, you can fit the posts into metal spike post supports which are simply hammered into the ground. The posts fit into sockets in the tops of the spike supports. In this case, 24in (600mm) long spikes are suitable for fences up to 48in (1200mm); for fences up to 72in (1800mm) high use 30in (760mm) long post supports.

The metal post supports are driven into the ground with a scrap of loose-fitting fence post in the socket to protect the socket from sledge hammer blows, keeping a check with a carpenter's level on all sides of the socket that the spike is going straight into the ground. You will also be able to push on the spike to correct any tendency for it to go into the ground out of plumb (vertical). Stretch a horizontal string line along the line of the proposed fence to ensure the metal spikes are driven into the ground in line and to the same height.

If you do not use metal post spikes, it is possible on soft ground to sharpen the ends of the posts into spikes and simply hammer them into the ground. However, using this method usually makes it difficult to get the posts absolutely in line and vertical, and it is better to dig a hole for each post using a metal post-hole digger, which can be rented. This hand-operated tool removes a plug of soil to leave a neat circular hole about 9in (225m) in diameter, and up to 24in (600mm) deep.

Posts can then be stood in the holes, lined up against a string line, and their heights adjusted to bring them all level by packing the holes as necessary. The posts are held upright by ramming gravel around them, and finally topping off with a collar of concrete around the post at ground level to throw rain-water clear of the post.

PREPARING AND AFFIXING POSTS

If you decide to point the posts to drive them into the ground (see above), the joints can then be cut with the posts in position. In all other cases it is better and easier to cut the joints with the post on a bench.

Hold a side rail flush with the top of the post and mark its depth on the post. Repeat for the other side of the post, and notch out 1in (25mm) wide recesses to the depth of the rails at the top of each post (fig. 1).

Position the posts by either dropping them into metal post support sockets or setting them into the ground, adjusting them to the same height. Place a long, straight batten across the post tops or post support sockets and use a carpenter's level to check that they are level.

If using metal post supports, screw or clamp the post bottoms into the supports. If placing posts in holes in the ground, pack around them with gravel and a concrete collar. Double check that all posts are in line, that they are vertical, and that the tops are level.

AFFIXING TOP RAILS

Anchor the top rails to the posts using two lag screws each side.

If it is necessary to join two rails, cut the rails to coincide with a post position and make a spliced joint (fig. 2). To maintain the strength of the fence, you should have only one spliced joint per post, staggering them from side to side.

At the fence ends, cut the rails flush with the edge of the post.

TOOLS

WORKBENCH (fixed or portable)
STEEL MEASURING TAPE
TRY SQUARE
SMALL CROSSCUT SAW (or circular saw)
TREE-PRUNING SAW
HAMMER
DRILL (hand or power)
DRILL BIT – $\frac{1}{4}$in (6mm)
WRENCH
CARPENTER'S LEVEL
CHISEL
MALLET
BILLHOOK (or ax or sharp knife)

MATERIALS

Part	Quantity	Material	Length
POSTS	As required	3 × 3in (75 × 75mm) sawn and treated softwood	As required*
RAILS	As required	1 × 3in (25 × 75mm) sawn and treated softwood	As required
BATTENS	As required	1 × 1$\frac{1}{4}$in (25 × 32mm) sawn and treated softwood	As required
CAPPING BOARD	As required	1$\frac{1}{2}$ × 3in (38 × 75mm) sawn and treated softwood	As required
BEANSTICKS	As required	Hazel, birch, or chestnut	As required

* Post length will depend on the height of the fence and whether you are inserting posts into the ground or into metal spike post supports

AFFIXING BOTTOM RAILS

The bottom rails are screwed to the outsides of the posts about 6in (150mm) up from ground level. Install a lag screw at one end of the rail, and use a carpenter's level to get the rail level before drilling and screwing the other end into another post. Use two lag screws per post, and make spliced joints if necessary to coincide with post positions.

Measure the distance between the posts and cut pieces of $1 \times 1\frac{1}{4}$in (25×32mm) roofing batten to fit snugly between them (fig. 3). Fit the battens inside the bottom rails, flush with the top edge, with the narrower edge toward the rails. Drive four galvanized screws through the bottom rails and into each batten. The battens create a gap about $\frac{1}{2}$in (12mm) wide between the bottom rails.

Repeat all along the fence.

If you plan to paint or stain the frame of the fence, do this now.

INSTALLING BEANSTICKS

Measure the distance from the top of the top rail to the bottom of the bottom rail, and cut all the beansticks to this length. They will tend to clog the saw teeth, so use a tree-pruning saw for this job.

Use a billhook, ax, or sharp knife to sharpen one end of each of the beansticks so that they wedge into the gap between the battens.

Starting at one end, feed the sticks in through the gap at the top of the frame and wedge them into the gap at the bottom, bunching them tightly until the frame is filled.

Trim all the beansticks flush with the top of the top rails. Press each stick down firmly as you cut it.

Finally, nail the capping board along the top of the fence, making sure it covers the edges of the top rails. If you cannot buy a capping board, you can cut one from a length of sawn wood. Paint or stain it to match the fence frame.

BEANSTICK FENCE ASSEMBLY

CAPPING BOARD

TOP SIDE RAIL

LAG SCREWS

BEANSTICKS

BATTENS

BOTTOM SIDE RAIL

POST

SECTION VIEW

① Affixing Top Rails
Notch out 1in (25mm) recesses to depth of side rail on sides of post at top. Screw rails to post.

② Joining Lengths of Rail
Join rails at post positions, if necessary, cutting rails at an angle to form spliced joint.

③ Affixing Beansticks
Sharpen one end of stick to a point and feed through top to wedge between bottom rail battens.

PART 5

CONTAINERS

Every year at Versailles, it takes the army to bring in the lemon and orange trees for the winter, hundreds of planted tubs comprising what must be the ultimate container garden. Container gardening is not usually on such a grand scale, but in every garden there is a place for at least some plants in pots, whether a pair of bay trees in formal tubs flanking an entrance, a collection of simple terracotta bowls tumbling with flowers, or cheerful hanging baskets providing a splash of summer color.

The versatility of container gardening is one of its main advantages: you can match plants exactly to their soil requirements, and place them where they will look most effective. If the container is not too large, you can move it to a position of prominence when the plant is in bloom. Planters and window boxes are excellent woodworking projects, allowing you to tailor-make your containers to suit their location exactly. If you use the same type of containers inside and out, group pots around entrances, on either side of French doors and on window sills you will create views which will help to dissolve the boundary between your house and the garden.

CONTAINERS

There are many advantages to gardening in containers. Usually, little or no weeding is required, which saves considerable maintenance time for people with only a few hours to spare. Compost and soil can be tailored to the precise needs of the plant, enabling a far greater range of species to be grown in the same location. Plants can also be arranged to suit the demands of the garden design, or to give shape to a flat landscape. You can also furnish an area with plants which might otherwise be barren, such as in the dry shade under a tree or on a roof.

Some plants positively flourish in containers. Figs, for example, like to be contained; a considerable number of other species can live undisturbed for many years in pots. Growing untidy and invasive herbs, such as mint, in containers also benefits the rest of the garden.

If containers provide a quick and easy way of creating a garden, they are also flexible enough to accommodate and express a whole range of garden styles. Containers are often associated with formal garden designs. Symmetrical arrangements of tubs, clipped box in painted wooden planters, and stone urns at the end of walkways or in the center of radiating beds are all ways of using containers to emphasize the geometry or architectural quality of a garden design.

However, containers can also be delightfully informal. Mediterranean gardens and terraces often feature large terracotta pots carefully positioned to make punctuation points in the overall design. In many Italian and Greek villages, painted and planted oil cans crowd windowsills and balconies, adding a jolt of color to the elevations of houses. Window boxes or hanging baskets spilling over with vivid geraniums and lobelia also work well in country locations or cottage-style gardens.

POTS OF PLANTS

Container gardening is flexible and provides an instant garden for a small space. Tubs or pots flanking an entrance are a common feature of formal garden designs, but can work well combined with less structured planting (above left). A variety of species can be grown in containers; you can train climbers to grow up purpose-built trellis from a tub (above) and even grow small trees (right).

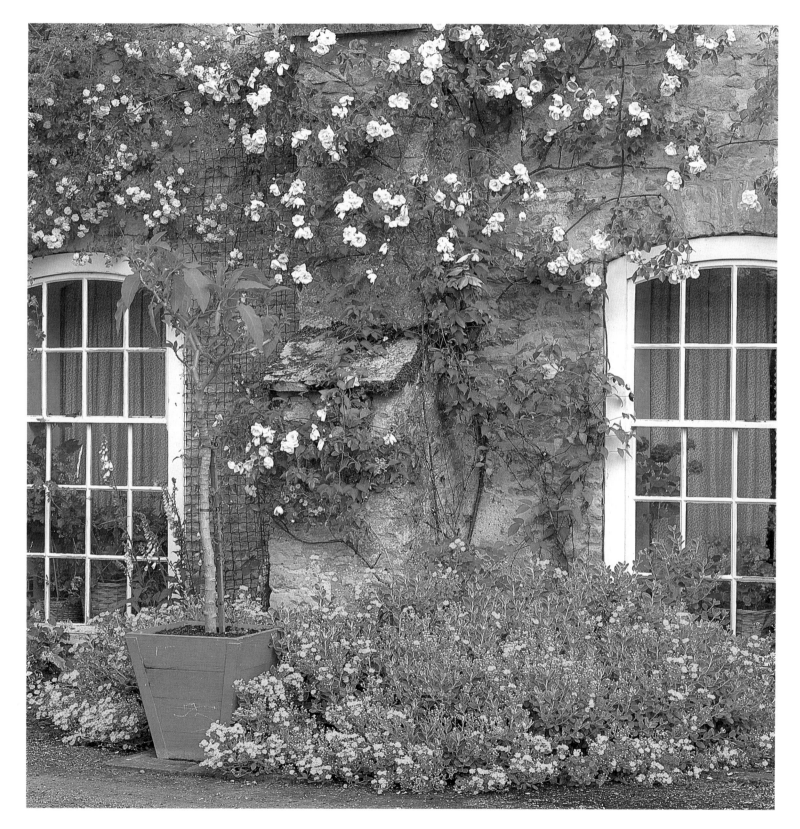

CONTAINERS

Whatever the overall style of the garden, containers should be used in a positive way. Place them to create a focal point, in the center of planting, or arrange a series of pots asymmetrically to lead the eye on through the garden. Containers can also introduce changes of height if they are placed on top of a wall or hung from the side of a house, an important consideration if the rest of the garden is fairly flat. You can also delineate an enclosed area or patio with a row of pots or planters, or make a special feature of an entrance by flanking it with a pair of tubs.

Wherever possible, mass containers in groups for increased effect, rather than dot them about the garden where their impact will be lost. You can group pots on metal garden staging which looks very attractive positioned at either side of a door, or adopt one solution seen on a French roadside, where the entire length of a garden wall was lined in shelves, set about 18in (45cm) apart, on which were arranged dozens of planted pots.

Plants should be massed in much the same way, although filling a container with a single variety is often more effective than a careful composition of a small amount of different species. Wooden boxes simply planted with box and ivy provide a graphic line of green at the window and require little maintenance to remain attractive and flourishing.

As far as the container itself is concerned, material, size, and style vary tremendously. Wherever possible, keep to natural materials – stone, wood, and terracotta all look marvelous and age in a sympathetic way. Metal containers, especially when made of lead, zinc, or copper, can be attractive and even rubber – in the form of old tractor tires – can be effective, contributing textural interest. Avoid plastic: it always looks glaringly out of place in a garden; its harshness

seems to stem from the fact that, unlike everything else, it does not weather or change, and usually has no texture.

In terms of size, choose containers which are on the generous side. Small pots will be overlooked and tend to have a prissy appearance which is at odds with the robust and striking effects you should be trying to create.

Ready-made containers include a range of plain terracotta shapes from urns to shallow bowls, from traditional flowerpots to troughs. Simple reconstituted stone containers can also look good, particularly if you encourage a little weathering. Wooden planters and tubs available commercially can be customized by staining or painting them to blend in with your house or to make a vivid color accent. Wooden containers are also, of course, a natural choice and suit a variety of different applications. A wooden tub is an excellent container home for small trees and shrubs, and half a wooden barrel is a classic. Wooden troughs or planters also make excellent raised beds, a practical and enjoyable way of gardening for older people or those with limited physical strength. Planting does not necessarily have to be at a low level in a container: a pyramid of bamboo sticks tied together and placed in a pot and planted with scarlet-flowering runner beans is a colorful and lovely sight!

One of the most appealing features of container gardening is the scope for improvization and humor in the choice of container. In this area, more than any other, there is great opportunity for creative salvage. Everything from half-barrels to old watering cans can be used as a plant container. Old sinks, wash tubs, chimney pots, and stone troughs can all be recycled to great effect, and architectural salvage yards can be a tremendous source of objects in this respect.

POTTED PLANTS

One of the most important advantages of container gardening is its ability to establish a visual connection between the house and garden. The current popularity of the conservatory bears out the common desire of people to include a sense of the outdoors in their homes. An array of the same type of containers can be used indoors and outside to create views that dissolve the boundary between house and garden.

COMPOST BIN AND PLANTER

The compost bin and planter are very similar in construction, made from rough-sawn boards affixed to posts. The simple nature of the design and lack of precision required in the finishing mean that these two structures offer a good means of practicing your woodworking skills and gaining the confidence to move on to more elaborate projects.

A compost bin is an invaluable asset for the gardener, providing a supply of rich organic matter which makes all the differ-ence to the way plants grow. At the same time, recycling your garden and kitchen waste is environmentally beneficial and economically sound.

The front posts of the bin are doubled up, making a slot where boards can be dropped into place as the pile builds up, or easily removed as the compost is taken out. It is worth buying "pressure treated" wood – compost is both hot and wet, so the wood needs the maximum degree of protection.

The planter provides a support for young trees, many of which either blow over or suffer from "windrock," instabi-lity of the root structure where growth stops and starts rather than proceeding at an even pace. The cross supports enable the trunk to be secured firmly in place while the tree becomes established.

The planter is painted with a coat of black tar to preserve the wood. Lag screws are used to bolt the boards to the uprights, giving a smart finishing touch.

COMPOST BIN

The principle of construction for the compost bin is the same as for the planter (pages 135–7). It is made from fencing-quality sawn and pre-servative-treated lumber.

The size of the bin can be varied to suit the site, but it should not be too large, since air will not be able to get to the center of the heap, hindering the production of good garden compost.

Our bin is about 36in (915mm) square. The height can also be altered according to your own requirements, but you should work in multiples of 5½in (137mm) – the depth of the 6in (150mm) boards after they have been planed – plus an allowance for ventilation gaps between the boards. Our bin is about 39in (990mm) high. Bear in mind that you want a height at which it will be comfortable to tip garden waste into the bin. Also, the heap does not want to be too high or you will not be able to climb onto the heap to tread down the waste material. Opinion varies on the optimum size for ventilation gaps; we suggest ½–¾in (12–19mm).

CONSTRUCTION

Cut all of the components to the lengths specified in the Materials chart below. The posts are left long and are cut down to size after the boards have been affixed to allow for the ventilation gaps between the boards. The bin is held together with lag screws, and C-clamps are useful for holding the boards squarely in place while they are being attached. The lag screw heads are a decorative feature of this compost bin, and it is important that they line up with each other and are the same distance in from the corners.

At the front of the bin, the only fixed board is at the bottom. The other retainer boards slot into the groove between the posts and are built up to the height required. They are therefore easily removed to gain access to the bin contents when the time comes to fork out the rotted compost.

MATERIALS

Note: All lumber is sawn and preservative-treated softwood

Part	Quantity	Material	Length
"LONG" BOARDS	9	1 × 6in (25 × 150mm)	36in (915mm)
"MIDDLE" BOARDS	6	As above	35in (890mm)
"SHORT" BOARDS	4	As above	34in (856mm)
RETAINER BOARDS	6*	As above	As above
POSTS	6	2 × 2in (50 × 50mm)	48in (1220mm)
LAG SCREWS	100	Galvanized steel	$\frac{5}{16}$ × 2in (8 × 50mm)

* Cut 7 retainer boards if you want the boards at the front to be level with the boards at the side and back

TOOLS

WORKBENCH (fixed or portable)

STEEL MEASURING TAPE

STEEL BENCH RULE

TRY SQUARE

SMALL CROSSCUT SAW (or circular power saw)

MARKING GAUGE

POWER DRILL

DRILL BIT – approximately 6mm (¼in) diameter to drill pilot holes for lag screws

WRENCH

ONE PAIR OF C-CLAMPS

1 Securing the First Board to the Posts
A "short" length of board is secured to the two posts flush and square with the ends to form the bottom row of the back of the bin. Two lag screws at each end hold it in place.

2 Adding the Side Posts and First Retainer Board
A "long" board at both sides is screwed in place, flush with the ends of the posts. The first retainer board rests against the back of the front posts and is later screwed to the posts from behind.

COMPOST BIN ASSEMBLY

POST

MIDDLE LENGTH BOARD

LONG LENGTH BOARD

FIRST RETAINER BOARD

LONG LENGTH BOARD

SHORT LENGTH BOARD

MIDDLE LENGTH BOARD

LONG LENGTH BOARD

LAG SCREWS

VENTILATION GAP

LAG SCREW

LONG

MIDDLE

POST

POST

SHORT

PLAN VIEW

COMPOST BIN

SQUARING THE FIRST ROW

Start to form the back of the bin by laying two of the posts on a flat surface. Then lay a "short" length of board across them flush with the bottom ends of the posts, so the outer edges of the posts are 34in (865mm) apart (fig. 1, page 132).

Check that the board is square to one of the posts, then clamp it to the post. Drill pilot holes for two lag screws and insert the screws to affix the board to the post.

Use a second board at the other end of the posts to ensure that they are square to the "short" length of board, then double-check that the post is square to the first board using a try square. Drill pilot holes for the two lag screws to be inserted into the other end of the first board, the same distance in as the lag screws at the other end.

Stand the frame upright and place a "long" board along the side, flush with the post, and secure it to the post with a C-clamp. Pilot drill and screw it to the post using two lag screws centered on the post.

Repeat for the other side with another "long" length of board.

Place another post inside this board flush with the end, check that it is square at the top using another "long" board, and screw into the post through the side board using two lag screws as before.

Take a retainer board and place it on the inside of the front posts (fig. 2, page 132).

BUILDING UP THE ROWS OF BOARDS

Place spacing blocks or a spacing batten about $\frac{1}{2}$–$\frac{3}{4}$in (12–19mm) thick on top of the back board, then lay a "long" length of board across the top (fig. 1). Check that it protrudes an equal distance beyond the outside edges of both the posts, then affix it in place with two lag screws at each end as before. For neatness, make sure that the lag screws line up with those on the board in the row below.

Repeat the process with one "middle" length board on each side; these should both fit flush with the ends of the back board.

Continue working in this way, one row at a time so that the back boards run alternately with "short"/ "long" lengths, and the sides with "long"/"middle" lengths to the height required. Ours is six boards high plus spaces.

As you work it is important to check that the structure is square by holding a spare board at the top flush with the posts each time a new board is added.

THE FRONT

With the bottom board at the front, screw through into the back of the front posts using two lag screws at each end.

Place the final two posts in position behind the lag screw heads, leaving at least a $\frac{1}{2}$–$\frac{3}{4}$in (12–19mm) gap from the front board to create a slot in which the retainers will be a very loose fit. Hold a post in position on the side boards using a C-clamp, then mark a vertical line on the outside of the boards for the lag screw positions (fig. 3).

Screw through each board into the post from the outside using two lag screws per board. Repeat for the post on the other side.

Drop the retainer boards into the slots created by the two posts on each side, building the retainers up to the height required. If you want the retainers to finish level with the boards at the sides and back, rip cut the top one to size.

Finally, cut off the tops of the posts so that they are flush with the top edges of the boards.

Place the bin in an appropriate site away from general view. Almost all types of organic matter can be used for producing compost, although anything too bulky should be avoided because it will slow down the rate at which composting takes place. Similarly, large quantities of leaves also tend to slow the process, and are best kept to decompose separately. Farmyard manure, on the other hand, will accelerate production, and it is a good idea to add a layer of manure or proprietary compost accelerator to your bin every 5–8in (125–200mm). Climate will affect when your compost will be ready.

1 **Building Up the Rows of Boards**
Use spacing blocks or a spacing batten to allow for ventilation gaps when affixing subsequent boards to the back and sides. Alternate "short" and "long" boards at the back, "long" and "middle" boards at the sides.

2 **Back Corner Detail**
Saw the posts so they are flush with top boards. Note that lag screws line up for a neat appearance.

3 **Forming the Front Slot**
A second post each side is screwed 1½in (38mm) behind front posts and retainer boards drop in place.

PLANTER

This planter allows you to grow trees, roses, shrubs, and other flowers where normally you would not be able to, such as on a paved patio or on a concrete path or driveway. The planter is made from fencing-quality sawn and preservative-treated wood. Since the finished planter would be too heavy to lift, there is no need for a floor panel – the planter is placed where required, the planting compost is added and the tree or shrub is planted. There is normally room for other plants around the edge, which will enhance your display.

The size of these planters can be varied according to your specific needs – ours is 30in (760mm) square and 30in (760mm) high, which is good for medium-size trees. For smaller shrubs and flowers you can make smaller planters, and if these are of a size that will still be light enough to move when planted, then it is worth putting a floor panel in the planter so that you can reposition it at will (see **Making a Floor Panel, page 137**).

The corner posts are extended upward and are joined at the top by two cross pieces which form a useful tree support. Omit the cross pieces and cut shorter posts if making a smaller model just for plants. The planter is held together with lag screws, and it is important that these neatly align with each other.

POSTS – CUTTING THE TOP JOINTS

Cut the corner posts to length, and then use the clean sawn end of the post to mark out the top joint for housing the cross supports. Place the edge of a length of 1 × 3in (25 × 75mm) lumber (cut from 1 × 6in [25 × 150mm]) centrally on the post end at a 45° angle and mark its position (fig. 1).

Place the cross support $\frac{1}{8}$in (3mm) down from the top of the post, ensure it is at right angles, and mark off the bottom edge. Square around on all four faces, then mark lines down the sides of the post from those drawn at the top.

Cut down the marked lines on each side of the post with a back saw and use a coping saw to remove the center section.

Repeat for other three posts.

MATERIALS

Note: All lumber is sawn and preservative-treated softwood

Part	Quantity	Material	Length
"LONG" BOARDS	10	1 × 6in (25 × 150mm)	30in (760mm)
"SHORT" BOARDS	10	As above	28in (710mm)
CORNER POSTS	4	2 × 2in (50 × 50mm)	53in (1350mm)
CROSS SUPPORTS	2	1 × 6in (25 × 150mm) cut to 1 × 3in (25 × 75mm)	48in (1220mm) cut to length as required
LAG SCREWS	80	Galvanized steel	$\frac{5}{16}$ × 2in (8 × 50mm)

TOOLS

WORKBENCH (fixed or portable)

STEEL MEASURING TAPE

STEEL BENCH RULE

TRY SQUARE

COMBINATION SQUARE – for marking 45° angles

SMALL CROSSCUT SAW (or circular power saw)

BACK SAW (or power saber saw)

COPING SAW

MARKING GAUGE

POWER DRILL

DRILL BIT – approximately 6mm ($\frac{1}{4}$in) diameter to drill pilot holes for lag screws

WRENCH

ONE PAIR OF C-CLAMPS

HAMMER – if fitting floor panel

1 **Marking Top Joint on Posts**
Mark cross support centrally on post end at 45°. Gauge lines down post to marked position and remove center.

2 **Securing the Second Frame to Form Main Construction**
Affix "short" boards flush with the ends of two lots of two posts. Screw "long" boards to the sides of one frame, then place the second frame inside the "long" boards so that the ends are square and flush.

PLANTER

MAIN CONSTRUCTION

Lay two of the corner posts on a flat surface and place a "short" length of board across them flush with the ends so that the outer edges are 28in (710mm) apart.

Secure the board to the posts by drilling two pilot holes at one end, about 1in (25mm) from the end, and screw in two of the galvanized lag screws. For a neat finish try to ensure that each lag screw is the same distance from the edge.

Hold a spare board at the other end to make sure that the post is square, double check using a try square and secure the opposite end of the first board in the same way, drilling the holes the same distance in from the outside edge.

Repeat the process with the other two posts, affixing a "short" board between them at the base.

Stand one of the frames upright, and place a "long" length of board along the side flush with the post and secure it in place using a C-clamp. Pilot hole and screw to the corner post with two lag screws centrally on the post. Repeat for the other side of the frame, using a "long" length of board as before.

Place the other frame inside these "long" boards, with the corner posts on the inside (fig. 2, page 135). Affix the sides to the corner posts with two lag screws each side.

BUILDING UP THE ROWS OF BOARDS

Take another "short" length of board and place it on top of the attached "long" board so its ends are flush with the posts. Clamp the board to the posts using a pair of C-clamps and affix it with two lag screws at each end, aligning them with the screws on the board below.

Take a "long" length of board and place it on the adjacent side so it overlaps the end of the "short" board (fig. 1). Make sure the end is flush; screw it into the corner post.

Continue in this way, one row at a time, so that the "short"/"long" boards run alternately, and ends are visible on each side on alternate rows. Build to five boards high (or whatever height you have decided on). It is most important to check that the structure is square as you work: do this by holding a board at the top flush with the posts each time a board is added.

AFFIXING THE CROSS SUPPORTS

Measure diagonally across the corner posts at the top of the planter and add 2in (50mm) so that there will be an overhang at each end. Cut two lengths to this measurement from 1 × 3in (25 × 75mm) stock.

At the middle of these two cross supports, cut two cross lap joints (see **Techniques, page 152**) and slot together. Fit the cross supports into the slots in the corner posts and glue them in place (fig. 3).

Unless you wish to color the wood there is no need to apply a special finish, as preservative-treated lumber is used for this project. If you

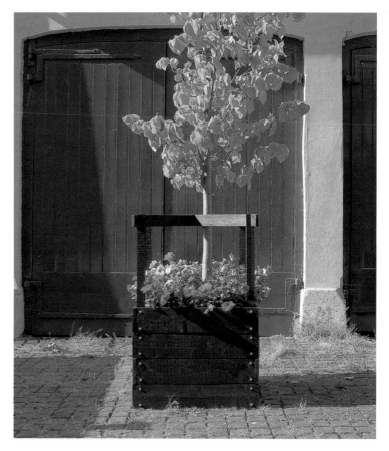

1 Building Up the Sides of the Planter
Build up the rows one at a time, affixing "short" boards above "long" boards and vice versa. Always check boards are square with the frame and ends are flush before screwing in place. Align screws with those on the boards below.

2 Joining the Cross Supports
Cut cross lap joints in the middle of the two cross supports so that they slot together.

do want to change the color of the wood, at this stage apply a water-repellent preservative wood stain of the desired shade. To avoid getting stain onto the lag screw heads, push lengths of plastic or rubber tubing over the heads before staining the planter.

MAKING A FLOOR PANEL

If a floor panel is required, screw 2 × 2in (50 × 50mm) battens to the inside of the planter at the base. Lay 1 × 6in (25 × 150mm) boards across the planter, resting on the battens. Space the boards so that there are narrow gaps about $\frac{1}{8}$in (3mm) wide between them to allow drainage of excess water. To assist the base in supporting a heavy weight of soil, you can reinforce it with additional 2 × 2in (50 × 50mm) battens spaced about 9in (225mm) apart under the floor panel and running at right angles to it.

Move the planter to the chosen site before adding the soil and planting the tree or shrub. A layer of small stones at the bottom of the planter will assist drainage.

❸ Affixing Supports to Posts
The cross supports fit into the slots cut in top of each post and protrude an equal distance. Glue in place.

PLANTER ASSEMBLY

CROSS SUPPORT

POST

LONG BOARD

SHORT BOARD

LAG SCREW

SHORT BOARD

LONG BOARD

COLD FRAME

If you can't afford a greenhouse, a cold frame is the next best thing. Most important for raising seedlings or growing early vegetables, it can also be used to provide salad ingredients such as lettuce all through the winter: a year-round usage which makes it an invaluable addition to any garden. If you do have a greenhouse, a cold frame can still be used to harden off bedding plants that have been raised in the greenhouse and as a place for overwintering delicate biennials.

The design of this cold frame varies little from the traditional version which is such a common garden sight. Extremely versatile and very simple to make, the wooden base is treated with exterior-grade preservative, contrasting with the crisp, white painted "light" or glazed lid. An important feature of the design is the ability to remove the entire light so that there is free access to the area of ground covered by the cold frame, enabling it to be dug over and planted easily.

Cold frames are best sited in south-facing positions where they will receive maximum sunlight, but, because they are usually portable, the position can be varied from year to year. If there is a danger of scorching at the height of summer, the glass may need to be coated with white "obscuring paint."

Unlike traditional cloches or glass bell-jars, a cold frame can be made simply and economically to provide a versatile extension of the growing season.

Cold Frame

TOOLS

WORKBENCH (fixed or portable)

STEEL MEASURING TAPE

STEEL BENCH RULE

TRY SQUARE (or combination square)

SMALL CROSSCUT SAW (or circular power saw)

BACK SAW

MARKING GAUGE

POWER DRILL

DRILL BIT – approximately ⅛in (3mm) diameter

COUNTERSINK BIT

SCREWDRIVER

CLAW HAMMER

NAILSET

PLIERS

CHISEL – about 1in (25mm)

MALLET

BAR CLAMPS (or folding wedges)

MATERIALS

Quantities are for the three-bay frame illustrated

Part	Quantity	Material	Length
FRAME STRUCTURE			
BOTTOM RAILS	4	2 × 2in (50 × 50mm) sawn and treated softwood	48in (1220mm)*
FRONT POSTS	4	As above	10½in (270mm)*
BACK POSTS	4	As above	16in (400mm)*
TOP RAILS	4	As above	48½in (1230mm)*
TOP SUPPORT BATTENS	6	1 × 1in (25 × 25mm) S4S softwood	48½in (1230mm)
FRONT JOINING BATTENS	6	As above	13in (330mm)*
BACK JOINING BATTENS	6	As above	18in (460mm)*
FRONT & BACK CLADDING	As required	¼ × ¾ × 6in (6 × 19 × 150mm) bevel clapboarding	Width of glazing frame plus clearance
END CLADDING	As required	As above	44in (1120mm)
GLAZED LIGHTS			
SIDE RAILS	6	1½ × 2in (38 × 50mm) S4S softwood	50in (1270mm)
TOP RAILS	3	As above	31½in (800mm)
BOTTOM RAILS	3	1 × 3in (25 × 75mm) S4S softwood	31½in (800mm)
CENTRAL GLAZING BARS	3	1 × 1½in (25 × 38mm) S4S softwood	50in (1270mm)
GLASS SUPPORT BATTENS – LONG	12	½ × 1in (12 × 25mm) S4S softwood	46in (1150mm)*
GLASS SUPPORT BATTENS – SHORT	6	As above	16in (400mm)*
GLASS SHEETS	18	Approx. 17 × 16in (425 × 400mm) clear glass	

Also required: 3 D-handles; metal glass clips; mastic for bedding glass; glazier's points for holding glass in place; glazed light supports

* Leave overlong and then cut to size after affixing – see text

A cold frame will be appreciated by all keen gardeners, whether their speciality is flowers, fruit, or vegetables. The frame will be useful for seedlings, propagation, and for growing delicate or early plants.

Our frame has been developed from the tried and tested standard cold frame that has evolved over the years. The main frame is made from sawn and preservative-treated softwood, put together in a series of inset "bays" clad with bevel clapboarding affixed between the main frames. This gives the frame a distinctive style and avoids the bland appearance of a conventional cold frame. However, you may prefer to run the clapboards along the whole length of the frame, which is quicker and easier.

The size of the frame from front to back and end to end is optional and can be varied as you wish according to what you want to grow. Our frame is a good average size, being 14½in (370mm) high at the front, 20in (500mm) high at the back, and 48in (1220mm) from front to back. The beauty of this design is that you can have a single section, or make a block of two, three, or more. We have built a three-section frame, and quantities in the Materials chart are for a frame of this size.

The glazed lights in our design are loose, giving flexibility in use. You have the option of sliding them back a little way for ventilation, farther back to tend for plants within the frame, or they can be lifted at the front and propped open a little way for ventilation. Alternatively, they are easy to slide off, either from the front or the back, allowing them to be removed completely. However, you could glaze the lights with sheets of clear plastic, which is also a safer option if young children play in the garden. In this case, you would affix the lights at the back with hinges; you will need a 2 × 3in (50 × 75mm) wood rail along the back, level with the support battens.

COLD FRAME ASSEMBLY

SIDE RAIL

GLASS SUPPORT BATTEN

END JOINING BATTEN

BOTTOM RAIL

CLAPBOARDS

FRONT POST

FRONT JOINING BATTEN

TOP RAIL

CENTRAL GLAZING BAR

GLASS SHEET

TOP RAIL

BACK JOINING BATTEN

BACK POST

20in

TOP SUPPORT BATTEN

48in

36in   14½in

FRAME STRUCTURE

MAKING THE DIVIDERS

The ground frame structure is built around four dividers (if you are making a three-bay cold frame), and construction starts with these. Start by cutting out the four components of the dividers – the top and bottom rails, and the front and back posts – from 2 x 2in (50 x 50mm) sawn softwood all at least 2in (50mm) overlong.

Lay the bottom rail down and mark off its final length centrally on one side. Place the front and back posts in position alongside.

Mark off the final heights of the front and back posts, and then lay the top rail alongside these top marks (with the correct post heights on the outer edges of each) so that the correct angles to cut the tops of the posts can be marked. Cut the posts to length.

Nail up the frame by toe-nailing through the bottom and top rails into the front and back posts.

Once the frame has been finished, check it for square, then cut off the "horns" (protruding ends) of the top and bottom rails so they are flush with the posts. Make up the required number of frame dividers – four in our example.

SUPPORT AND JOINING BATTENS

Place an offcut of the 1½ x 2in (38 x 50mm) glazing frame side rail, 1/16in (2mm) down from the upper edge of the top rail to position the top support battens. You will need one on each side of the central dividing frames and on the inner sides of the end frames. Nail them in place, then saw the ends flush with the front and back posts.

Unless you are nailing the cladding in continuous lengths to the front and back of the dividing frames, you will need to nail joining battens to the front and back posts.

Hold the battens in place so that the tops can be marked at the angle of the top support batten. Cut the battens to this angle, then screw them in place so that they are flush with the inside edges of the front and back posts (fig. 1, page 142). Saw the ends of the battens flush with the bottom edge of the bottom rail. Affix side battens on both sides of the dividing frames, and on the inner sides of the end frames.

To support the cladding at the ends, measure internal heights of the front and back posts on the end frame. Cut battens to these lengths and affix to the inside edges of the end frames (fig. 2, page 142).

COLD FRAME

GLAZED LIGHTS

Cut out all the components. Each glazed light frame will require two sides, one top rail, one bottom rail, and one central glazing bar (fig. 3).

Mark out all the joints as shown (fig. 3). The sides are joined to the top rail using corner half-lap joints (*see* **Techniques, Half-lap joint, page 152**). The bottom rail is lapped onto the sides so that the bottom rail is on the underside.

The glazing bar is joined to the top rail with a T-half-lap joint and to the bottom rail with a lap joint on the *opposite* side (the underside) so that it laps onto the bottom rail as shown (fig. 3).

Letter all the joints clearly to identify them for assembly, and then cut them all out.

MAKING UP THE GLAZED LIGHT FRAMES

Glue all the joints to the top and bottom rails, starting with the central glazing bar. Use a waterproof woodworking adhesive such as epoxy resin. Turn the frame over so that it can be screwed together from the underside. Use a try square to make sure that the frame is square, and hold it with clamps to keep the joints tight while drilling two pilot holes and a countersink for each of the three top joints. Screw the top joints together.

Drill and screw the bottom corner joints with three screws each. Measure to check that the central glazing bar is central on the bottom rail, then drill two holes and screw the bar to the bottom rail.

Lay the frame on a flat surface and check it is square by measuring the diagonals. Then nail on a bracing batten to keep the frame square while the glue is drying. Clean off any excess glue with a damp cloth and leave the joints to dry.

Repeat the process for the required number of frames – in this case three.

GLASS SUPPORT BATTENS

Cut four lengths of $\frac{1}{2} \times 1$in (12 × 25mm) batten to the internal length of the glazing frame and nail them so that they are flush with the underside of the frame.

Then cut two lengths to the internal widths between the side battens at the top. Nail the battens at the top between the two pairs of side battens, with the lower edge flush with the underside of the frame.

Repeat for the other frames.

CLADDING

Although we used bevel clapboarding for cladding the frame, other cladding boards could equally well be used – for example, shiplap, tongue-and-groove, or V-jointed.

For the sides, cut the cladding to the internal dimensions of the end frames. Affix the cladding, working up from the bottom board, nailing into the joining battens. When using bevel clapboards, the cladding boards should overlap by about $\frac{1}{2}$in (12mm), and the nails holding the lower edge of each board should pass through the top edge of the board beneath to hold it securely. Use galvanized round head nails.

When affixing the end cladding, the top boards must be shaped to the slope of the top rail.

The front and back clapboards are cut to fit between the dividing frames so that the glazed frames, when fitted, will be a loose fit. You will need to leave enough clearance to allow for the wood to swell when it gets wet. Check that the main dividers are spaced so that there is about $\frac{1}{16}$in (2mm) of clearance between the dividers and the sides of the glazing frames so that they will slide in place easily.

Nail the bevel clapboards to the front and back joining battens, working up from the bottom boards as before. The upper corners at each end of the top boards will have to be notched out so that the clapboards will fit tightly around the top support battens.

If you are affixing the front and back cladding in a continuous strip, dispense with the front and back joining battens, and nail the clapboards directly to the front and back posts of the dividing frames. If the boards are of insufficient length to

① Fitting the Top Support Batten and Side Joining Battens
Left Detail shows spacing block held $\frac{1}{16}$in (2mm) down from top rail to position top support batten. *Below* Top support batten runs length of top rail; side joining battens fit flush with inside edges of front and back posts and are angled at top to fit beneath top support battens.

② Affixing End Battens
Cut end panel joining battens to internal heights of posts, and fit flush to inside edges of frame.

③ Making the Frames for the Glazed Lights
Top Corner half-lap joints fit side rails to top rail; T-half-lap joint fits glazing bar to top rail; lap bottom rail to underside of side rails and glazing bar.
Below Glue and screw from underside; bracing batten holds frame square.

clad the frame in continuous strips, shorter lengths of clapboards can be used: simply butt joint them together so that the joint coincides with the midpoint of a front or back post. Stagger these joints so they do not line up with joints in boards directly above or below.

PRESERVING AND FINISHING OFF

It is most important to treat the whole of the frame assembly with at least two coats of clear or colored wood preservative. When dry, this can then be painted with a microporous or exterior gloss paint, or it can be treated with a water-repellent preservative stain if a natural wood color is required. You must not use creosote or any wood preserver that is harmful to plants.

FITTING THE GLASS, HANDLES, AND HINGES

Have the glass cut to fit the glazed frames. We had ours cut in three sheets on each side, with the bottom sheet feeding first and subsequent sheets overlapping the previously affixed sheet. The bottom sheet is held by small aluminum clips, nailed to the bottom glazing frame rail and

bent back over the edge of the glass to prevent it from slipping out. All the sheets are bedded into mastic on the glazing support battens. The glass sheets are held with small nails, called glazier's points, nailed into the side rails so that they are horizontal and hold the glass down. The bottom edges of the overlapping sheets of glass rest against two glazier's points which prevent the sheets from sliding down.

As an alternative to glass, the lights can be glazed with clear plastic sheeting, which is cheaper and much safer. Make sure that you buy purpose-made horticultural plastic which will encourage the plants to thrive and will also prevent premature yellowing and cracking of the plastic. Do *not* buy plastic containing an ultra-violet (UV) inhibitor as nothing will be able to grow in the cold frame.

To make it easier to lift the glazed lights for ventilation and access to the plants, screw a D-handle into the bottom end of the glazing bar.

If the glazed lights are left loose, they can be lifted at the front edge and wedged open with a wooden block for ventilation; the lights can also be slid backward or forward to gain access to inside the frame.

Alternatively, the glazed lights can be hinged at the back, and this is a particularly good option when the lights are glazed with plastic and are therefore lighter. In this case, cut a 2 × 3in (50 × 75mm) batten to the total length of the frame and bevel the top edge to allow the glazed light to fold back beyond 90° (so that it will rest open against a wall or fence behind the frame). With the batten level with the top support battens, screw it to the back posts. Then screw hinges into the back edges of the glazing frames, and into the top edge of the beveled batten (*see* **Techniques, page 152**).

A simple ventilation prop can be made simply from a 2 × 4 × 6in (50 × 100 × 150mm) wood block

with 1in (25mm) steps cut along one edge to allow variable ventilation up to 6in (150mm). Another method is to install a swing-down prop to hold the glazed light partially open. The prop can be affixed to the underside of the central glazing bar and held out of the way in a tool clip when not in use.

If the frame is glazed with plastic lights and hinged at the back, affix hooks and eyes to the front edge of the frame to hold the lights firmly closed in windy conditions.

The frame should be positioned in a sunny place, and can simply be rested on the soil. Alternatively, you could place it on a partially buried row of bricks which will help to keep the wood dry. If the frame is to be permanently sited, it should be placed on a strip of damp-proofing placed on two rows of bricks over a concrete foundation (to act as a vapor barrier). Affix the frame using expansion bolts inserted into the brick foundation through the bottom rails, or use metal strips screwed to the foundation and to the inside of the frame structure.

④ Glass Support Battens
Cut side battens to internal lengths of frame and top battens to internal length between side battens.

TOOLS, MATERIALS, AND TECHNIQUES: TOOLS

TOOLS FOR PREPARATION

Adjustable T- bevel This is a type of square used to mark out timber at any required angle.

Bench stop and vise A vise is fitted to the underside of a bench, the jaws level with the bench top. The jaws are lined and topped with hardwood to protect the work and any tools being used. Some vises incorporate a small steel peg (a "dog") that can be raised above the main jaw level. This allows awkward pieces of wood to be clamped in position when used with a bench stop fixed at the opposite end of the bench.

Drill stand Enables a power drill to be used with extreme accuracy when, for example, dowel jointing. The hole will be perpendicular to the surface and its depth can be carefully controlled. The drill is lowered onto the work with a spring-loaded lever which gives good control.

Marking gauge This is used to mark both widths and thicknesses with only a light scratch. The gauge comprises a handle, on which slides a stock bearing a steel marking pin which can be fixed at a precise point.

Mortise gauge Similar to a marking gauge, it has two pins, one fixed, one adjustable, to mark out both sides of a mortise at the same time.

Utility knife Used to score a thin line for a saw or chisel to follow, ensuring a precise cut.

Miter box A simple open-topped wooden box which is used to guide saws into materials at a fixed 45° or 90° angle, to ensure an accurate cut.

Plumb bob and chalk Used to check or mark accurate vertical lines on walls. A plumb bob is simply a pointed weight attached to a long length of string. The string can be rubbed with a stick of colored chalk to leave a line on the wall.

Portable workbench A collapsible, portable workbench is vital for woodworking. It is light-weight and can be carried to the job, where it provides sturdy support. A portable bench is like a giant vise – the worksurface comprises two sections which can be opened wide or closed tightly according to the dimensions of the work and the nature of the task.

Carpenter's level Used for checking that surfaces are horizontal or vertical. A 24in (610mm) long level is the most useful size. An aluminum or steel level will withstand knocks and it can be either I-girder or box-shaped in section. A 9in (225mm) "torpedo" carpenter's level is useful for confined spaces and can be used with a straight-edge over longer surfaces.

Steel measuring tape A 12ft (3.6m) or 18ft (5.5m) long, lockable tape (metal or plastic) is best, and one with a top window in the casing makes it easier to read measurements.

Steel bench rule Since the rule is made of steel, the graduations are indelible and very precise. A rule graduated on both sides in imperial and metric is the most useful. The rule also serves as a precise straight-edge.

Straight-edge Can be made from a length of 1 × 2in (25 × 50mm) scrap wood. It is used in combination with a carpenter's level to tell whether a surface is flat and also for checking whether two points are aligned with each other.

Try square An L-shaped precision tool comprising a steel blade and stock (or handle) set at a perfect right angle to each other on both the inside and outside edges. Used for marking right angles and for checking a square.

Combination square A versatile measuring and marking tool comprising a steel ruler, try square, miter square, and carpenter's level.

TOOLS FOR SHARPENING AND CUTTING

Chisels Used to cut slots in wood or to pare off thin slivers. Some chisels may be used with a mallet when cutting slots. When new, a chisel's cutting edge is ground and must be honed with an oilstone to sharpen it before use.
Mortise chisel Used for cutting deep slots.
Firmer chisel For general-purpose use.
Bevel-edge chisel Used for undercutting in confined spaces.
Paring chisel Has a long blade for cutting deep joints or long grooves.

Doweling jig Clamps onto a piece of work, ensuring that the drill is aligned over the center of the dowel hole to be drilled.

DRILLS

Hand drill For drilling holes for screws or for making large holes, particularly in wood. It will make holes in metal and is useful where there is no power source. A handle attached to a toothed wheel is used to turn the drill in its chuck.
Power drill These range from a simple, single-speed model (which will drill holes only in soft materials) to a multi-speed drill with electric control. Most jobs call for something in between, such as a two-speed drill with hammer action.

DRILL BITS

You will need a selection of drill bits in various sizes and of different types for use with a drill.

Auger bit Has a tapered, square shank that fits into a carpenter's brace. It is used to make deep holes in wood, the usual lengths being up to 10in (250mm). Diameters range from $\frac{1}{4}$in (6mm) to $1\frac{1}{2}$in (38mm). The tip has a screw thread to draw the bit into the wood.
Countersink bit After a hole is drilled in wood, a countersink bit is used to cut a recess for the screwhead to sit in, so ensuring that it lies below the surface. Different types are available for use with a carpenter's brace or a power drill.
Brad-point bit Used to make dowel holes. The top has two cutting spurs on the side and a center point to prevent the bit from wandering off center.
Forstner bit Primarily used for boring flat-bottomed holes to accept the hinge bosses on concealed hinges. Forstner bits are used in electric drills, ideally fitted in drill stands, and should be set to drill no deeper than $\frac{1}{2}$in (12mm).
Spade bit Is used with a power drill. For maximum efficiency the bit must be turned at high speed from about 1000 to 2000 r.p.m. It drills into cross grain, end grain, and man-made boards.
Masonry bit Has a specially hardened tungsten-carbide tip for drilling into masonry to the exact size required for an anchor. Special percussion drill bits are available for use with a hammer drill when boring into concrete.
Twist drill bit Used with a power drill for drilling small holes in wood and metal.

Power router This portable electric tool is used to cut grooves, recesses, and many types of joints in lumber, and to shape the edge of long lumber battens. A range of cutting bits in different shapes and sizes is available and when fitted into the router the bits revolve at very high speed.

SAWS

Back saw For cutting the tenon part of a mortise and tenon joint, and for other delicate work. It has a stiffened back and the blade is about 10–12in (250–300mm) long.

Circular saw For cutting large pieces of wood or sheets of board, as well as grooves and angles. The most popular size has a diameter of 7¼in (184mm). Circular saws can be extremely dangerous and must be used carefully. The piece of work must be held securely, supported on scrap battens, and the blade depth set so that it will not cut into anything below the work. The tool should be fitted with an upper and a lower blade guard.

Compass saw Has a narrow, tapered blade to cut holes and shapes in wood. A hole is drilled and the saw blade is inserted to make the cut.

Coping saw Used to make curved or circular cuts. It has a narrow blade, which can be swiveled. When cutting, the blade can be angled so that the frame clears the edge of the work.

Hacksaw For cutting metal. A traditional hacksaw has a wooden handle and a solid metal frame. The blade is tensioned by a wing-nut. Modern hacksaws have a tubular frame which is adjustable for different lengths of blade.

Hand saw A saw used for rough cutting rather than fine carpentry. It has a flexible blade of 20–26in (510–660mm).

Saber saw More versatile than a circular saw, although not as quick or powerful. It cuts curves, intricate shapes, angles, and holes in a variety of materials. Good models offer variable speeds.

Rasp A coarse file, available with flat or half-round surfaces, used to shape wood.

Surforms Available in a range of lengths from approximately 6–10in (150–250mm), these rasps are useful for the initial shaping of wood. The steel blade has a pattern of alternating small teeth and holes through which waste wood passes, so that the teeth do not get clogged up.

HAND TOOLS

Abrasive paper *see* Sanding block

CLAMPS

For securing glued pieces of work while they are setting. There are many types of clamp, but the C-clamp is the most commonly used and is available in a wide range of jaw sizes.

C-clamp Also called a frame clamp or fast-action clamp, it is important for our projects that the jaws of the clamp open at least 8in (200mm). The wood to be held in the clamp is placed between the jaws which are then tightened by turning a thumb-screw, tommy bar, or other type of handle. With a fast-action clamp, one jaw is free to slide on a bar, and after sliding this jaw up to the workpiece, final tightening is made by turning the handle. To protect the work, scraps of wood are placed between the jaws of the clamp.

Bar clamps These employ a long metal bar, and are indispensable for holding together large frameworks, although you can improvise in some cases by making a rope tourniquet. This consists of a piece of rope which is tied around the object, and a length of stick to twist the rope and so clamp the frame tightly.

Band clamp The webbing, like narrow seat-belt type material, is looped around the frame, pulled as tight as possible by hand, and then finally tightened by means of a screw mechanism or ratchet winder.

HAMMERS

Claw hammer The claw side of the head of the hammer is used to extract nails from a piece of work, quickly and cleanly.

Cross-peen hammer The peen is the tapered section opposite the flat hammer head, and it is used for starting off small brads and tacks.

Tack hammer A smaller version of the cross-peen; this is useful for light work.

Hand staple gun A trigger-operated tool which fires a staple straight into a surface, usually fabric, fiberboard, or thin wood over a wooden batten. Its advantage over conventional nailing with a hammer is that it is used one-handed.

Mallet Most commonly used to strike mortise chisels, although if a chisel has an impact-resistant handle then a hammer may also be used. The tapered wooden head ensures square contact with the object being struck.

Nailset Used with a hammer to drive nails and brads below the surface so that they are hidden and the holes can then be filled.

Orbital sander This gives a fine, smooth surface finish to wood. A gritted sanding sheet is fitted to the sander's base plate. Sheets are graded from coarse to fine, and the grade used depends on the roughness of the surface to be sanded. Orbital sanders produce a great deal of dust, so always wear a mask when using one.

Paintbrushes A set of paintbrushes for painting and varnishing should ideally comprise three sizes – 1in (25mm), 2in (50mm), and 3in (75mm). A better finish is always achieved by matching the size of the brush to the surface – a small brush for narrow surfaces, a large brush for wide areas.

PLANES

Block plane Held in the palm of the hand, it is easy to use for small work and chamfering edges. Also useful for planing end grain.

Jack plane A good all-purpose tool with a long blade used for straightening long edges.

Power plane Finishes lumber to precise dimensions. A one-hand model is lightweight and can be used anywhere, whereas the heavier two-hander is intended for workbench use. A power plane will also cut bevels and rabbets.

Smoothing plane A general-purpose, hand-held plane for smoothing and straightening surfaces and edges. The plane is about 10in (250mm) long and its blade 2–2¼in (50–60mm) wide. The wider the blade the better the finish on wide lumber. There is a fine adjustment for depth of cut and a lever for lateral adjustment.

Sanding block and sandpaper A sanding block is used with sandpaper to finish and smooth flat surfaces. The block is made of cork, rubber or softwood and the sandpaper is wrapped around it. Make sure that the paper is not wrinkled. Coarse paper is used for a rough surface and fine paper for finishing.

Screwdrivers Come in many shapes and sizes, the main differences being the type of tip (for slotted or Phillips screws), the length, and the shape of the handle, which varies from straight or fluted to bulb-shaped.

Ideally, you should have a range of screwdrivers for dealing with all sizes of screws. Ratchet models, which return the handle to its starting point, are easy to operate since your hand grip does not need to change.

Wrench A wrench is required for tightening carriage bolts, and any type that fits the head of the bolt is suitable. If the correct-size open-ended or ring wrench is not available, any type of adjustable wrench may be used.

Materials

Lumber and Sheet Boards

Lumber This is classified into two groups – softwoods and hardwoods. Softwoods come from evergreen trees and hardwoods from deciduous trees. Check your lumber for defects before buying it. Avoid wood which is badly cracked or split, although you need not be concerned about fine, surface cracks since these can be planed, sanded, or filled. Do not buy warped wood, as it will be impossible to work with. Check for warping by looking along the length of a board to see if there is any bowing or twisting.

Wood for outdoor projects must be protected from rot and insect attack. It can be bought pre-treated with preservative, but this is expensive and not always readily available. Alternatively, you can buy untreated wood and treat it, as soon as possible, with one of the finishes described here. Pay special attention to end grain and to posts which will be buried below ground – a double coating is a good idea here.

Softwood Softwood is much less expensive than hardwood and is used in general building work. Softwood is sold either by the *lineal* foot or the *board* foot. The former is based on the length of a piece of wood – for example, 8ft of 1 by 2 (1 × 2in [25 × 50mm]). The board foot is calculated by the thickness in inches × width in feet × length in feet – for example, 10ft of 1 by 6 would be 5 board feet: 1in × $\frac{1}{2}$ft (6in) × 10ft.

It is important to remember that standard softwood sizes refer to sawn sizes – that is, how it is sawn at a mill. Sawn timber is suitable for most of the projects in this book. However, where a smooth finish is specified, where appearance and accuracy are important, it will need to be planed. Such wood is referred to as S4S (smooth 4 sides), and, since planing takes a little off each face, it is $1\frac{1}{4}$–$\frac{3}{4}$in (6–19mm) smaller in width and thickness than stated.

Hardwood Expensive and not as easy to obtain as softwoods, hardwoods often have to be ordered or bought from a specialist lumberyard. Many lumberyards will machine hardwood to your exact specification.

Sheet boards Mechanically made from wood and other fibers, they are versatile, relatively inexpensive, made to uniform quality and available in large sheets. You need to know the advantages of each type before making your choice.

Plywood Made by gluing thin wood veneers together in plies (layers) with the grain in each ply running at right angles to that of its neighbors. This gives it strength and helps prevent warping. The most common boards have three, five, or seven plies. Plywood is graded for quality: N is perfect, followed by A, B, C, and D in decreasing order of quality. Usual thicknesses of plywood are $\frac{1}{8}$in, $\frac{1}{4}$in, $\frac{1}{2}$in, and $\frac{3}{4}$in (3mm, 6mm, 12mm, and 19mm). WBP (weather and boil proof) grade board must be used for exterior work.

Lumber core Made by sandwiching natural lumber strips between wood veneers, the latter usually of Far Eastern redwood or plain birch. Although plain birch is a little more expensive than redwood it is of a much better quality. Lumber core is very strong, but can leave an ugly edge when sawn, making edge fixings difficult. Lumber core is graded in the same way as plywood and common thicknesses are $\frac{1}{2}$in, $\frac{3}{4}$in, and 1in (12mm, 19mm, and 25mm).

Tongue-and-groove boarding Also called match boarding, or matching, this is widely used for cladding frameworks. The boarding has a tongue on one side and a slot on the other side. The tongue fits into the slot of the adjacent board; this joint expands and contracts according to temperature and humidity without cracks opening up between boards. Make sure you use exterior grade boarding for outdoor projects.

Bevel clapboards These taper from a thick edge across to a thin edge. When fixed in place, the thick edge of one board overlaps the thin edge of the next board.

Adhesives and Fillers

Adhesives Modern adhesives are strong and efficient. If they fail, it is because the wrong adhesive is being used or the manufacturer's instructions are not being followed carefully. For outdoor woodworking, you must always use either a synthetic resin adhesive that is mixed with water (this has gap-filling properties, so is useful where joints are not cut perfectly) or a two-part epoxy resin adhesive where the parts are applied separately to the surfaces being joined.

Fillers For outside work, always use an exterior grade filler which has been specially formulated to withstand the natural movement of cracks and holes caused by weather changes.

If the wood is to be painted over, use an exterior painter's caulk. This dries white and will be evident if used under any other kind of finish. When a clear finish is needed, fill cracks and holes with a proprietary wood filler. These are thick pastes and come in a range of wood colors. You can mix them together or add a wood stain if the color you want is not available. Choose a color slightly paler than the surrounding wood, since fillers tend to darken when the finish is applied. Some experimentation may be needed on a waste piece of matching wood.

Finishes

The choice of finish is determined by whether the wood or board is to be hidden, painted, or enhanced by a protective clear finish.

Paint A liquid gloss (oil-based) paint is suitable for wood, and is applied after undercoat. Generally, two thin coats of gloss are better than one thick coat. Non-drip gloss is an alternative. It has a jelly-like consistency and does not require an undercoat, although a second coat may be needed for a quality finish. If you intend to spray the paint, you must use a liquid gloss.

Microporous paint This is applied directly to the wood – neither primer nor undercoat is needed. The coating will not flake or blister as the special formulation allows trapped moisture to evaporate. If applied over old gloss paint, it will lose the quality that prevents flaking or blistering.

Preservative Unless wood has been pre-treated with preservative and it is not to receive an alternative decorative finish, you must use a coat of preservative. Modern water-based preservatives are harmless to plant life. They are available in clear, green, and a number of natural wood colors. The preservative sinks well into the wood, preventing rot and insect attack.

Varnish For outdoor use, you must always use an exterior grade varnish – stated on the container – or a yacht varnish. It is available as a gloss, satin, or matt finish, all clear. Varnish also comes in a range of colors, so that you can change the color of the wood and protect it simultaneously. The color does not sink into the wood, so if the surface becomes scratched or marked then its original color will show through. A wood stain or dye can be used to change the color of wood. It sinks into the wood, but offers no protection, so varnish is also needed.

CONCRETE

Concrete Made by mixing Portland cement and ballast (a mixture of sand and aggregates) with water. The usual mix for paths, bases, and foundations is one part cement to four parts ballast. Although concrete mix is available dry-mixed in bags, this is economically viable only for small jobs. Concrete can be mixed by hand, but it is an arduous task, and it is advisable to rent a small electric mixer.

Precast concrete pavers These come in a range of shapes and sizes with 18in square (450mm square) being the most popular, since anything larger is difficult to handle. There is a limited range of colors, and surface finishes are smooth, patterned, or textured. Thicknesses are usually about 1½in (35–40mm).

Bricks and **Mortar** *see* **Techniques: Bricklaying, pages 156–7**

DIVIDERS

Required principally to mark boundaries and to create privacy and security. Among the most popular types of fences are:
Vertical board A solid, secure fence which can be of any height. Beveled boards are nailed to horizontal rails which, in turn, are secured to wood or solid concrete posts.
Waney-edged panels Pre-fabricated panels made from larch or pine planks which overlap horizontally. The panels are normally 72in (1800mm) wide and 24–72in (600–1800mm) high, and are fixed to wood or concrete posts.
Palisade Vertical timber pales (stakes) nailed to rails at 2in (50mm) intervals and in turn affixed to wood posts. Pales can have ornate or square tops. Heights vary, but 36in (900mm) is the most popular. Usually used for front yards.
Ranch-style Horizontal wood rails nailed at intervals to wood posts. A two-rail fence is usually about 39in (1000mm) high; a four-rail fence is about 51in (1300mm) high.
Chain link A secure fence, 36–144in (900–3600mm) high. The metal mesh can be galvanized or plastic-coated. Posts are either steel or concrete.
Plastic wire Ornamental fencing commonly used to mark a boundary or surround a fish pond or herbaceous border. The fencing can be put directly into the ground, but it should be affixed to posts if it is over 24in (600mm) high. It is sold in rolls and cut to the required length.

Rustic poles Hazel, birch, or chestnut poles are available from garden centers. Diameters range from 2–5in (50–125mm). You will need the larger sizes for main uprights and bearers and the thinner ones for cross beams. The poles have bark attached; this will peel off in time.

Trellising Square trellis (lattice) is available in panel heights from 24–48in (600–1220mm) and in 72in (1800mm) long sections. The squares are each about 6in (150mm) and the trellis is made from hardwood battens. Diamond trellis comes in heights from 12–48in (300–1220mm) and lengths of 72in (1800mm).

FASTENERS

The choice of fastener depends on the size and weight of the materials being joined.

Nails For general-purpose frame construction.
Common nails With large, flat, circular heads, these are used for strong joints where frames will be covered, so that the ugly appearance of the nails does not matter.
Annular threaded nails Used where really strong attachments are required.
Round finishing nails Used when the finished appearance is important. The heads are driven flush with the surface of the wood.
Brads For attaching thin panels, these have unobtrusive heads that can be driven in flush with the wood's surface or punched below it.
Masonry nails For securing wood battens to walls as an alternative to screws and anchors.

Screws All types of screws are available with conventional slotted heads or with Phillips heads. The latter are the best type to use if you are inserting screws with an electric screwdriver.

For most purposes, screws with countersunk heads are ideal as the head lies flush with the surface after insertion. Round-head screws are for affixing metal fittings such as door bolts, which have punched-out rather than countersunk screw holes. Ovalhead screws are used where a neat appearance is important.
Wood screws These have a length of smooth shank just below the head. This produces a strong clamping effect, but there is a possibility of the unthreaded shank splitting the wood.
Twin-threaded screws Less likely to split wood than wood screws. Except for larger sizes, they are threaded along their entire length, giving an excellent grip in wood and sheet boards.

Lag screws For heavy-duty fastening when making frameworks requiring a strong construction. The screws have square or hexagonal heads and are turned with a wrench. A washer is used to prevent the head cutting into the wood.

Anchors Use a masonry drill bit to drill a hole which matches the size of screw being used (a No. 10 bit with a No. 10 screw, for example). Insert the plug in the hole, then insert the screw through the object being fixed and into the anchor.

Wall anchor bolt Similar to an anchor, but with its own heavy-duty machine screw. You need to make a larger hole in the wall, typically ⅜in (10mm) in diameter. The anchor sleeve expands in the hole as the bolt is tightened.

Expansion bolt This comprises a segmented body which expands as the bolt inside it is tightened. The body grips concrete, brick, or stone securely. There are various lengths and diameters and there are also versions containing a hook or an eye. Most bolts are galvanized, but aluminium bronze versions are available where greater resistance to corrosion is required.

Corrugated fasteners For strengthening glued joints in frameworks. Sizes are $\frac{1}{4}$–$\frac{7}{8}$in (6–22mm) deep and $\frac{7}{8}$–1$\frac{1}{4}$in (22–30mm) long.

Staples A useful means for quickly anchoring plastic mesh fencing to timber posts.

Battens A general term used to describe a narrow strip of wood. The usual sizes are 1 × 1in (25 × 25mm) or 1 × 2in (25 × 50mm).

Battens can be screwed to a wall to serve as bearers for shelves or they can be affixed in a frame on a wall, with sheet material or boards mounted over them to form a new "wall".

Dowels Used to make framework joints or to join boards edge-to-edge or edge-to-face.

Hardwood dowels are sold in diameters of $\frac{1}{4}$in, $\frac{3}{8}$in, and $\frac{1}{2}$in (6mm, 9mm, and 12mm). Dowel lengths should be about one-and-a-half times the thickness of the boards being joined.

Dowels are used with adhesive and, when the joint is complete, it is important to let excess adhesive escape from the joint. Dowels with fluted (finely grooved) sides and beveled ends will help this process. If you have plain dowels, make fine sawcuts along the length yourself.

TECHNIQUES: SAWING AND CUTTING

MEASURING AND MARKING SQUARE

Mark the cutting lines lightly with a hard pencil first, and then use a utility knife, straight-edge, or try square along a steel rule to create a sharp, splinter-free line.

To mark wood square, use a try square with the stock (handle) pressed against a flat side of the wood, called the face side or face edge. Mark a line along the square, using a knife in preference to a pencil, then use the square to mark lines down the edges from the face mark. Finally square the other face side, checking that the lines join up right around the wood.

If you are measuring and marking a number of pieces of the same length, then clamp them together and mark across several of them at the same time.

SPACING BATTEN

This is simply an offcut of wood, about ¾in or 1in square (19mm or 25mm square), which is used to ensure that any slats to be affixed across a frame are spaced an equal distance apart. To ascertain the length to cut the spacing batten, simply bunch all the slats at one end of the frame. Measure to the other end of the frame and divide by the number of spaces (which you can count while you have the slats laid side by side). The resulting measure is the length to cut the spacing batten, which is used to position each slat exactly.

BRACING

When making a frame, it is vital that it should be square, with corners at perfect right angles. You can ensure this using one of two methods.

3-4-5-method Measure three units along one rail, four units down the adjacent rail, then nail a bracing batten accurately to one of the unit marks. Pull into square so that the bracing batten measures five units at the other unit mark, forming the hypotenuse of the triangle. Saw off the batten ends flush with the frame, but do not remove the batten until the frame is fitted in place.

Try square method Nail a batten into one rail, pull into square by using a try square, and then nail the batten into the adjacent rail.

MAKING FOLDING WEDGES

Folding wedges are very useful for clamping large frames on a bench top during assembly. The wedges are always used in pairs, but more than one pair may be used to hold a large framework.

Make each pair of wedges from a piece of lumber (hardwood is an ideal material for this) measuring 1½ × 1½ × 13in (38 × 38 × 330mm). Make the wedges by sawing the lumber diagonally into two pieces.

To use the wedges, a wooden batten is first nailed to the bench and the item to be clamped is placed against the batten. Another batten is nailed to the bench, parallel with the first, and about 1¾in (45mm) away from the item. The wedges are now placed between the item and the second batten. Next, the ends of the wedges are knocked inwards with two hammers, thereby clamping the frame.

SAWING AND CUTTING

Cross-cutting to length by hand Hold the lumber firmly with the cutting line (see **Measuring and Marking Square,** above) overhanging the right-hand side of the bench (if you are right-handed). With the saw blade vertical and the teeth on the waste side of the line, draw the handle back to start the cut. To prevent the saw jumping out of place, as you start hold the thumb joint of the other hand against the side of the saw blade.

Rip-cutting by hand With the lumber or board supported at about knee height, start the cut as described above, then saw down the waste side of the line, exerting pressure on the down cut only. If the saw blade wanders from the line, clamp the edge of a wood batten exactly above the cutting line on the side to be retained, and saw along it.

Using a portable power saw If the cutting line is only a short distance from a straight edge, adjust

---

① Marking Lumber to Length and Square All Around
Mark across the face of the lumber with a utility knife held against a try square blade. Move knife around corners and mark sides, and finally mark other side to join up the lines.

② Using Spacing Battens
Measure distance from bunched slats to frame end. Divide by number of spaces to calculate batten size.

③ Making Folding Wedges
Saw wood diagonally. Nail batten to bench; wedges fit between batten and item being clamped.

the saw's fence so that when it is run along the edge of the lumber, the blade will cut on the waste side of the cutting line. If the lumber is wide, or the edge is not straight, clamp a batten to the surface so that the saw blade will cut on the waste side of the line when run along the batten.

Ensuring a straight cut When cutting panels or boards using a power circular saw or Saber saw, the best way to ensure a straight cut is to clamp a guide batten to the surface of the work, parallel with the cutting line, so the edge of the saw sole plate can be run along the batten. The batten position is carefully adjusted so that the saw blade cuts on the waste side of the cutting line. Depending on which side of the cutting line the batten is clamped, when using a circular saw, it is possible the motor housing will foul the batten or C-clamps used to hold it in place. In this case, replace the batten with a wide strip of straight-edged plywood clamped to the work far enough back for the motor to clear the clamps.

④ **Cross-cutting to Length**
Hold the lumber firmly. Steady the saw blade with the thumb joint as you start to saw.

⑤ **Straight Power-saw Cutting**
Top Use the rip fence of the saw if cutting near the edge. *Above* Cutting alongside the batten as a guide for obtaining a straight cut.

⑥ **Cutting with a Back Saw**
Start the cut as for a hand saw. As the cut progresses keep the blade horizontal.

CUTTING A CIRCLE

With a coping saw Mark out the circle, score the cutting line, and drill a hole about ⅜in (10mm) in diameter just on the inside of the circle. Disconnect the blade from one end of the frame, pass the blade through the hole, and re-connect it to the frame. It will be best to clamp the piece of work vertically when cutting the circle. The blade can be turned in the frame to help the frame clear the piece of work, but even so, with a coping saw you will be restricted in exactly how far you are able to reach away from the piece of work. If the circle is some way from the edge, use a compass saw to cut it.

With a compass saw A compass saw, similar to a keyhole saw, has a stiff, triangular pointed saw blade attached to a simple handle. A very useful saw blade is available for fitting in a regular knife handle.

Because this saw has no frame, it is ideal for cutting circles and other apertures, like keyholes, anywhere in a panel.

⑦ **Straight Rip-cutting**
Clamp a straight batten alongside the cutting line and saw beside the batten. A wedge holds the cut open.

Preparation of the circle for cutting is the same as for a coping saw. When cutting with a compass saw, keep the blade vertical and make a series of rapid, short strokes without exerting too much pressure.

CUTTING GROOVES

By hand Start by marking out the groove with a utility knife. Hold the piece of work on a bench and, with a back saw, make vertical cuts just inside the marked lines to the depth of the groove. If the groove is wide, make a series of other vertical cuts in the waste wood. Now chisel out the waste, working from each side to the middle. Finally, with the flat side of the chisel downwards, pare the bottom of the groove so that it is perfectly flat.

With a router Use a straight-sided router bit set to the depth required for the groove. Ideally, the bit should be the exact width of the groove. Make the cut along the waste side of the line with a batten clamped in place to guide the base of the router.

⑧ **Cutting Circles by Hand**
1 Drill a small hole and cut circle using a compass saw. *2* Making the cut with a coping saw.

TECHNIQUES: DRILLING AND FASTENINGS

CUTTING RABBETS

A rabbet is an L-shaped step in the edge of a piece of wood.

By hand Use a marking gauge to mark the rabbet width across the top face of the piece of work and down both sides. Mark the depth of the rabbet across the end and sides.

Hold the wood flat and saw down on the waste side of the marked line to the depth of the rabbet. Chisel out the waste one bit at a time along the end grain.

With a router It is not necessary to mark out the rabbet unless you want a guide to work to. However, do practice on scrap wood to be sure of setting the router correctly.

If using a straight cutter, adjust the guide fence on the router so that the correct width is cut, then plunge and adjust the cutting depth so that the router will cut to the correct depth. When the router is correctly set up, simply hold it flat on the piece of work and move it against the direction of the cutter's rotation.

If you are using a cutter with a guide pin, simply adjust the depth of cut and then run the cutter along the edge of the wood to form the rabbet. The cutter will follow irregularities in the wood, so make sure your wood is perfectly straight.

PLANING

By hand Make sure that the plane blade is sharp and properly adjusted. Stand to one side of the work with feet slightly apart so you are facing the work. Plane from one end of the work to the other, starting the cut with firm pressure on the leading hand, transferring it to both hands, and finally to the rear hand as the cut is almost complete. Holding the plane at a slight angle to the direction of the grain can sometimes improve the cutting action.

With a power plane Remove loose clothing, and wear goggles and a dust mask. Clamp the work in place. Start the plane and turn the adjuster knob to set the depth. Start with a shallow cut and increase the depth if necessary.

Stand comfortably to one side of the work and, holding the plane with two hands, set it into the work at one end and pass it over the surface to the other end. When you have finished, switch off and make sure the blades stop spinning before resting the plane down with the cutting depth at zero.

DRILLING

To minimize the risk of splitting wood, drill pilot and clearance holes for screws.

The **clearance hole** in the wood should be fractionally smaller in diameter than the screw shank.

The **pilot hole** to receive the screw should be about half the diameter of the clearance hole. The hole depth should be slightly less than the length of the screw.

To ensure that screwheads lie level with the surface of plywood, particleboard and hardwood use a **countersink drill bit**.

Drilling vertical holes To ensure vertical holes, mount the drill in a stand. If this is not possible,

stand a try square on edge so that its stock is resting on the work alongside the drilling position, and the blade is pointing up in the air. Use this as a siting guide and line up the drill as close as possible with the square to ensure the drill is vertical. It is also helpful if an assistant can stand back and sight along the drill and square from two sides to ensure the drill is straight.

SCREWING

When screwing one piece of wood to another ensure that half of the screw penetrates through the bottom piece of wood. Its thickness should not exceed one-tenth of the width of the wood into which it has to be inserted. Keep screws at a distance of five times their shank diameter from the side edge of the wood, and ten times the shank diameter from its end.

NAILING

The correct length of nail to use is two-and-a-half to three times the thickness of the lumber being nailed. However, check that the nail

① Chiseling a Groove
After making saw cuts at side, chisel out waste from each side. Finally pare base flat.

② Drilling Vertical Holes
With a drill stand, not only will the drill bit be held vertical, but depth is also controlled.

③ Freehand Drilling Guide
When drilling it can be helpful to stand a try square alongside the drill to ensure accuracy.

④ Drilling Depth Guide
There are various guides to control drilling depths, such as rings for drills and masking tape.

will not pierce right through two pieces being nailed. Wherever possible nail through the thinner piece of wood into the thicker piece.

Nails grip best if driven in at an angle ("toe-nailing"). A row of nails should be driven in at opposing angles to each other. Framework joints are usually held in by toe-nailing. Clamp or nail a block of wood temporarily against one side of the vertical piece to stop it sliding as the first nail is started.

To prevent wood from splitting, particularly if nailing near an edge, blunt the points of the nails by hitting them with a hammer before driving them home. Blunt nails will cut through lumber fibers neatly, while pointed nails are more likely to push the fibers apart like a wedge.

FASTENINGS

Solid wall The normal attachment for a solid wall is a wood screw and plastic or fiber anchor. Before drilling the hole, check with a metal detector that there are no pipes or cables hidden below the surface. Drill the holes for the anchor with a

6 Toe-nailing for Strength
Hold the frames together in a clamp and join them by toe-nailing (driving nails at an angle). The joint will not then pull apart.

5 Drilling Holes for Screws in Lumber
Drill a clearance hole in the thinner piece. Countersink this hole, then drill a pilot hole to slightly less than screw length. *Inset* To counterbore, drill to the diameter of the screw head to required depth, then as above.

masonry drill bit in an electric drill. The anchor package will indicate the drill size to use. Switch to hammer action if the wall is hard. The screw should be long enough to go through the fixture and into the wall by about 1in (25mm) if the masonry is exposed, and by about 1¾in (35mm) if fastening into a plastered wall.

If the wall crumbles when you drill into it, mix up a cement-based plugging compound (available from home improvement stores). Turn back the screw half a turn before the compound sets (in about five minutes). When hard (in about one hour) the screw is removed and a heavy attachment made.

If your drill sinks easily into the wall once it has penetrated the plaster layer, and a light gray dust is produced from the hole, you are affixing into lightweight concrete blocks. In this case, special winged anchors should be used.

To make a quick, light-to-medium weight attachment in a solid wall, a masonry nail can be used. Choose a length that will penetrate the

material to be attached, and pierce an exposed masonry wall by ⅝in (15mm) or a plastered wall by about 1in (25mm). Wear goggles in case the nail snaps; hammer it gently through the material to be attached and into the wall.

Expansion bolts In rugged construction work, wall attachments are made with expansion bolts. The hole drilled in the wall must be deep enough to accept the segmented body of the bolt. Check the manufacturer's instructions for the exact diameter of the hole. The body of the bolt is placed in the hole, the bolt passed through the fixture to locate in the body, and then the nut of the bolt turned with a wrench, expanding the segmented body and causing it to grip tightly.

Installing cladding Always install boards from the bottom upwards. Use a carpenter's level to check that the first board is exactly horizontal – if it is not, the boards above will start to run out of true, making it impossible to secure them.

7 Techniques for Joining Wood by Nailing
Nails should be two-and-a-half to three times the thickness of the wood being joined. Assemble frames on bench by nailing against batten. *Inset* Blunt nail points to avoid splitting wood.

TECHNIQUES: WOOD JOINTS

Nail through the center of the first board into each of the vertical support battens behind, using 1in (25mm) galvanized common nails. If boards have to be joined to span the full width of the structure, then butt the edges closely and ensure that joints are always made against a vertical support batten.

If you are installing bevel clapboards, it is important that they overlap uniformly and you will need to use a spacing block cut from a spare piece of wood. If the boards are 6in (150mm) wide and the spacer is 4½in (112mm) wide then, by aligning the spacer with the bottom edge of the previously fixed board and resting the overlapping board on top, you will get a consistent overlap of 1½in (38mm). Nail through the lower edge into the top edge of the board it overlaps and through into the batten.

Tongue-and-groove boards are installed by driving the nail at an angle through the tongue and tapping the head below the surface. The groove of the next board slides over the tongue to conceal the nail.

Shiplap cladding is installed in the same way except that the boards do not interlock, but simply overlap.

Installing trellis Trellis should be affixed about 6in (150mm) clear of the ground so that it will not rot at the base. Stand the trellis on blocks of the correct height while it is being secured to wood uprights or a wall. Use a carpenter's level to check that the horizontal rails are true, then drill holes into the side uprights of the trellis through which galvanized nails are inserted and then driven into the posts behind. If you nail directly into the trellis there is a chance the wood will split. Three nails either side of an 72in (1800mm) high trellis panel will suffice. Alternatively, use purpose-made clips screwed to support posts. The trellis slots into clips.

When securing to a wall, use 1in (25mm) thick wood blocks behind each attachment point to keep the trellis clear. Pre-drill the holes and use about 3in (75mm) long No. 8 or 10 galvanized screws and anchors to secure the trellis.

Installing posts and poles On concrete paths and pavers laid on mortar you can use a steel base as an attachment point for posts. The base is a square plate with a projecting cup into which the post is located. The base is bolted in place.

Metal post spikes are driven into the earth. Again, the post fits into a square cup and is clamped in place. As the post is above ground it is far less susceptible to rotting at the base.

Posts and poles can be inserted directly into soil. In firm soil and where shorter posts are used, then well-compacted gravel is usually adequate support. In loose soil and for longer posts and poles, a combination of stones and concrete should be used. For a post 72in (1800mm) high, at least 24in (600mm) should be buried below the ground.

FITTING HINGES

Butt hinges These are conventional flapped hinges and are available in steel (commonly) or in brass, which is better for high-quality work.

They are relatively simple to install, except that the hinge flaps have to be recessed into the wood using a chisel or router.

Mark out the hinge positions on the frame of the item to be hung, making sure that the hinges are not positioned so that the screws will go into the end grain of cross members and be likely to pull out.

The length of the hinges is marked out first, using a utility knife, then the width of the hinge and the thickness of the flap are marked using a marking gauge. With a chisel held vertical, and a mallet, cut down around the waste side of the recess, then make a series of vertical cuts across the full width of the recess. Remove the waste by careful chiseling, then finally pare the bottom of the recess flat using the chisel held flat side downwards (fig. 4).

If you are careful, you can remove the bulk of the waste from a hinge recess using a straight bit fitted in a router. The bit is set to cut to the depth of the recess required, and afterwards the corners can be finished off using a chisel.

WOOD JOINTS

Butt joint This is the simplest frame joint of all. The ends of the wood to be joined must be cut square so that they butt together neatly. Corner and "T" joints can be formed, which are glued and nailed for strength. Corrugated fasteners can also be used to hold these joints, especially where the sides of the frames will be covered to hide the fasteners. When "T" joints are being formed from inside a frame, they can be toe-nailed.

Half-lap joint Also known as a halving joint, these may be used to join wood of similar thickness at corners or to "T" or "X" joints. The joint is formed by cutting each piece to half its thickness. Use a try square to mark the width of the cut-outs and a marking gauge set to half the

① Installing Cladding
Above Nail tongue, then slot groove of next board over. *Below* Use spacing block for bevel clapboards.

② Installing Posts
Left and top right Post spikes affix posts in place. *Below right* Post-hole digger makes hole for post.

③ Installing Trellis Panels
Panel clips are screwed to vertical support posts. Trellis panels slot into clips and are screwed in place.

thickness of the wood to mark their depth. Be sure to cross-hatch the waste wood with a pencil so that the correct side is removed. To form an end-lap joint, saw down as for making a tenon joint (*see* **page 154**). To form a "T" or "X" half-lap, saw down each side of the "T" cut-out to the depth of the central gauge line, then chisel out the waste.

Dado joint Used mainly for shelving, this is basically a slot into which a shelf fits. The "through" dado joint goes to the full width of the shelf, while a "stopped" dado joint is taken only part of the way across the board. Chisel the waste away from each side. In the case of a stopped dado, chisel the waste from the stopped end first. If you have a router, it is easier to cut a dado joint by running the router across the board against a batten which is clamped firmly at right angles to the board.

A rabbet joint is similar to a dado joint, but positioned at the top of a piece of board; it can be cut in a similar way.

④ The Stages in Fitting a Butt Hinge
Using a try square and a utility knife, mark out the length of hinge. With a marking gauge mark width and thickness of hinge flap. With chisel vertical, cut around outline of hinge. Make series of cuts across width of recess. Pare out the waste then check that flap lies flush. Screw the butt hinge in place.

⑤ Simple Butt Joints
Top Corner and *Below* "T" joints can be formed by toe-nailing or by using corrugated fasteners.

⑥ Types of Half-lap Joints
Top An end-lap joint. *Bottom left* A "T" half-lap joint. *Bottom right* A "X" half-lap joint.

⑧ Types of Dado Joints
Top A through dado joint; *Middle* Through dado joints on the side of a central support; *Bottom* A corner dado joint.

⑦ Forming a Half-lap Joint in Wood Battens
Mark width of the cut-out. Mark half the thickness of the wood with a marking gauge. Cross hatch area to be removed. Saw down sides with a back saw, then chisel out the waste.

TECHNIQUES: WOOD JOINTS

Dowel joint Dowels are a strong, simple, and hidden means of joining wood together.

Use pre-cut grooved dowels with beveled ends (*see* **Materials, page 147**). These range from ¼in (6mm) diameter by 1in (25mm) long to ⅜in (10mm) by 2in (50mm). The dowel length should be about one-and-a-half times the thickness of the wood being jointed. When making your own dowels, their length can be twice the thickness of the wood. Cut grooves down the length of dowel to allow glue and air to escape, and bevel the ends.

On both pieces of wood, use a marking gauge to find the center line, and mark with a pencil. Drill the dowel holes to half the dowel length with the drill held in a drill stand, or aligned with a try square stood on end. Drill the dowel holes in one of the pieces to be joined, insert center points in the holes, then bring the

1 Dowels to Join Panels
Right Mark dowel positions. Drill holes, insert center points. Mark second piece.

2 Types of Dowel Joint
Dowels can join panels edge to edge and join frames at corners. They can be hidden or have ends exposed.

3 Making a Doweled Frame
If edge of frame will not be seen, drill holes for dowels after making frame. Hammer dowels home; cut ends flush after glue dries.

4 Using a Doweling Jig
If dowels are to be hidden, a doweling jig makes it easy to drill holes that align in both pieces.

two pieces of the joint together so they are carefully aligned. The center points will make marks in the second piece of wood where the dowel holes should be drilled. Drill the holes to half of the length of the dowels, plus a little extra for glue. Where dowels are used for location rather than strength, set the dowels three-quarters into one edge and a quarter into the other.

Put adhesive in the hole and tap dowels into the holes in the first piece with a mallet. Apply adhesive to both parts of the joint; bring the pieces together and clamp them in position until the adhesive has set.

Using a doweling jig A doweling jig enables accurate dowel holes to be drilled. It is clamped over the workpiece above the pre-marked hole centers. A bush of the same diameter as the drill bit is selected and fitted on the jig. The bush holds the drill vertically as the hole is made. A depth gauge ensures that the hole is the required depth. The jig is then set up on the mating piece of wood and the process repeated.

Miter joint A simple miter joint is glued and nailed; a stronger one is made using dowels, or by sawing oblique cuts into which wood veneers are glued. Cut the joints at 45° using a miter box as a guide.

Mortise and tenon joint A mortise and tenon joint can be marked out with a mortise gauge. Mark out the tenon (the tongue) so that it is one-third of the thickness of the piece of wood. The mortise (the slot) is marked at the same width in the other piece. The length of the mortise should match the width of the tenon being fitted. Drill out most of the waste with a series of holes using a bit slightly smaller than the mortise width. Working from the center, chop out the mortise with a chisel to the depth required. If making a through joint (in which the end of the tenon is visible), turn the wood over and finish chiseling out the mortise from the other side.

Hold the tenon piece upright, but sloping away from yourself, secure in a vise, and use a back saw carefully to cut down to the shoulder. Then swivel the wood around to point the other way, and saw down to the other side of the shoulder. Next, position the wood vertically and cut down to the shoulder. Finally, place the wood flat and saw across the shoulder to remove the waste. Repeat for the waste on the other side of the tongue. Check that the two pieces fit well before gluing and assembling the joint. For added strength, cut small additional shoulders at each end of the tenon.

Bare-faced mortise and tenon joint If the tongue of a tenon joint is offset to one side, this produces a bare-faced tenon as shown (fig. 8). This produces a strong joint where narrow rails meet thicker frame rails.

A bare-faced tenon is cut in the same way as a half-lap joint.

⑥ Marking and Cutting a Mortise and Tenon Joint
Mark the length of the mortise slot to match the size of the rail being joined. Set the mortise gauge to the width of the chisel being used to cut out the mortise slot. (Chisel should be about one-third the width of wood being joined.) Use the mortise gauge to mark the mortise, and also the tenon, on the rail. Drill out the mortise and complete the cut with a chisel. Use a back saw to cut out the tenon.

⑤ Cutting Miter Joints
Miters make right-angled joints. Use a miter box to ensure a 45° angle and cut joint with a back saw.

⑦ Mortise and Tenon Joints
Top A common or stopped mortise and tenon joint. *Below* Through mortise and tenon joint.

⑧ Making a Bare-Faced Mortise and Tenon Joint
Tenon is offset to one side. Mark and cut as shown here.

⑨ Shouldered Tenon Joint
For enhanced strength, saw down small additional shoulders at each end of the tenon.

TECHNIQUES: BRICKLAYING

TOOLS

Bricklayer's chisel and hammer For cutting bricks.

Brick trowel Used to spread mortar on bricks.

Buckets You will need two of the same size, one for measuring mortar ingredients, the other for cement.

Builder's square Three battens in the proportions 3:4:5 nailed to form a right-angled triangle. Used to check that each course is vertical.

Hawk board For holding small amounts of mortar.

Mason's level For checking brickwork horizontally and vertically.

Pointing trowel Small trowel for shaping mortar joints.

Profile board Made from a piece of scrap wood about 20in (500mm) long, nailed across two battens which are driven into the ground. You will need two – one for either end of the wall. The top of each board is notched at appropriate intervals to represent the edges of the foundation and the wall. The notches then hold the string line taut for accurate bricklaying.

Shovels You will need two of these, one for mixing and one for lifting cement from its bag.

Story pole This is a 1 × 1in (25 × 25mm) batten marked off in 2¾in (70mm) increments. It is used to check that courses of bricks are vertical. It should be slightly longer than the intended wall height.

String line Needed as a guide to laying the brick courses horizontally.

Watering can For adding water to the mortar mix.

MATERIALS

Bricks Modular bricks are made to an actual size of 7⅝ × 3⅝ × 2¼in (190 × 96.5 × 60mm). Since allowance has to be made for ⅜in (10mm) thick horizontal and vertical mortar joints, they are regarded as being 8 × 4 × 2⅝in (200 × 100 × 65mm).

Bricks come in many colors, sizes, and textures, and it is important to choose a type that will harmonize with your garden and house. Second-hand bricks are popular for garden projects since they blend well with any environment. Lumberyards stock a selection of bricks; local demolition sites or architectural salvage yards are good hunting grounds for second-hand bricks.

Mortar This is needed to bond the bricks together. It is made by mixing cement, soft builders' sand, and lime or plasticizer in the proportions of 1:5:1 with water. Bags of ready-mixed mortar are available, but they are economical only for very small jobs such as repair work.

Ordinary Portland cement (sold in large bags) is usually used although white Portland cement is available if you want pale joints to match pale bricks.

Builders' sand is sold by the cubic yard (meter). Most lumberyards will sell smaller quantities in bags – larger quantities are tipped from a truck into a loose pile.

Lime is sold in bags, liquid plasticizer in containers.

When calculating how much to buy, a good rule of thumb is to allow one bag of cement and 0.2 cubic yards (meters) of damp sand for every 400 bricks.

Should you need to store cement before use, keep it under cover and raised off the ground. A pile of sand will attract children and animals, so cover this, too.

Mix mortar on a clean surface. In hot weather, mix only as much as you can use in an hour, since the mortar will start to stiffen. Never try to reactivate mortar by adding more water: it will crack up. On a hot day, it is worth dipping each brick in water before laying it.

First, mix the dry ingredients until the pile is a uniform gray colour. Make a crater in the top and pour in some water, then turn the pile over continuously, adding a little more water from time to time until the mix is buttery. A good test for the right consistency is to chop the mixing shovel through the pile until the ridges remain intact.

TECHNIQUES

Laying foundations Unless the brickwork is built on a firm base it will soon start to settle unevenly. Judging foundations is a matter of common sense, although you must check codes and regulations.

Whereas a low brick planter or barbecue can be built on a sound existing patio or drive, more ambitious projects require tailor-made solid concrete foundations. For a garden wall up to 39in (1000mm) high (two brick thickness), dig a trench 20in (500mm) wide and deep, and lay a leveled bed of concrete in the trench to a depth of 9in (230mm). For a single brick thickness wall, you will need to dig a

① Single Brick Foundation
Dig trench and lay concrete bed as indicated. Lay bricks and backfill with soil once mortar has hardened.

② Laying First Two Bricks
Lay first brick using profile board as guide. Lay second brick 60in (1500mm) away; check it is level.

③ Laying the Second Course
Begin with a half brick to stagger courses, then continue along. Always check bricks are vertical and level.

Mortar
Backfilled earth
Brick
Earth
14–16in
3in
Concrete
6in

Profile board
String lines
Mason's level
First brick
60in
Second brick

trench 12in (300mm) wide and 14–16in (350–400mm) deep, and lay a 6in (150mm) deep bed of concrete in the trench.

The concrete mix should be one part cement to four parts of ballast. Allow it to harden for four days and keep it covered with polyethylene in wet weather. In hot weather, cover the concrete with damp sacking, spraying it occasionally with water.

Cutting bricks To cut a brick, score a continuous line around all four faces using a bricklayer's chisel and hammer. Place the brick on a pile of sand, put the blade of the chisel in the groove, and tap sharply with the hammer for a clean cut.

Brickwork bonds For stability, a wall must be built in a definite bond formation such as one of the examples illustrated (fig. 7). Running and open bond formations are suitable for single brick thickness walls up to a height of 39in (1000mm). Piers (support columns), as indicated (fig. 5), are essential at both ends and at 72in (1800mm) centers.

A double brick thickness wall requires bricks to be cut near the corners to ensure that the vertical joints are staggered.

Laying bricks Set up string lines at either side of the foundation trench as a guide to laying the first course of bricks. Make profile boards from pieces of scrap wood notched as appropriate for a single or double brick wall – the notches trap the string, pulling it taut.

Spread a layer of mortar about 60in (1500mm) long and lay the first brick in place with the indentation facing upwards. Lay a second brick 60in (1500mm) or so away. Place a mason's level on a straight-edge piece of wood spanning the two bricks and tap the higher brick down until both are level.

Mortar should always be a little thicker than $\frac{3}{8}$in (10mm) since the bricks will compress it slightly.

As each brick is laid, spread $\frac{3}{8}$in (10mm) of mortar on the end to form a vertical joint with the preceding brick. Use the level and trowel to level bricks. Complete first course.

Cut a brick in half to start the second course. Build up the ends of the wall as shown (fig. 4), so that you are always working three or four courses above the course being filled. The course being completed must be laid to match against a taut string line which you will need to anchor into the course above using bradpoint nails.

Check continually with the story pole that the courses are accurate. Also check the face of the brickwork to ensure it is plumb.

The top course of bricks (the coping course) protects the wall from the weather. On a single brick wall, stand half bricks on edge. Whole bricks on edge complete a double thickness wall.

Joint finishes It is best to finish the joints as each course of bricks is completed. The simplest joints to make are flush joints, made by scraping away excess mortar using the edge of a trowel.

Beaded joints are more decorative and are made by drawing a steel rod through the mortar.

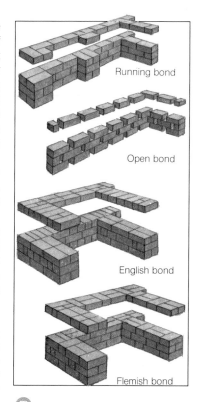

Running bond

Open bond

English bond

Flemish bond

7 Brickwork Bonds
Lay bricks to stagger with the course above and below. Four popular bond formations are shown here.

4 Laying Additional Courses
Build up the ends of the wall first, then fill in the intervening bricks, completing one course at a time.

5 Forming Piers
For long walls, stagger the brick formations as shown to form piers at centers 72in (1800mm) apart.

6 Forming the Ends
Use a combination of half bricks and whole bricks to form the bonding necessary at either end of the wall.

8 Cutting a Brick
Score line around faces of brick. Lay it on bed of sand, insert chisel in groove, tap sharply with hammer.

$\frac{3}{4}$ brick

$\frac{1}{2}$ brick

$\frac{3}{4}$ brick

Whole brick

Whole brick

$\frac{1}{2}$ brick

INDEX

ACKNOWLEDGMENTS

The publisher thanks the following photographers and organizations for their kind permission to reproduce the photographs in this book:

8 left Brigitte Thomas; **8** right Gary Chowanetz/ Elizabeth Whiting & Associates; **9** Lamontagne; **10** left Brigitte Thomas; **10** right Jerry Harpur/Conran Octopus (designer Tim Du Val); **11** left Marijke Heuff (designer K Noordhuis); **11** above right Brigitte Thomas; **11** below right Marijke Heuff (The Coach House – Little Haseley); **12** above left Lamontagne; **12** above right Ron Sutherland/Garden Picture Library (designer Rick Eckersley); **12** center left René Stoeltie; **12** center right Georges Lévêque; **12** below left Brigitte Thomas; **12** below right Arnaud Descat/Agence Bamboo; **13** above left Bent Rej; **13** above right John Glover/Garden Picture Library; **13** center left Lamontagne; **13** center right Lars Hallen; **13** below left Tim Street-Porter/Elizabeth Whiting & Associates; **13** below right Georges Lévêque; **14** left Gilles de Chabaneix for Terence Conran; **14** center Lamontagne; **14** right Gary Rogers/Garden Picture Library; **15** Brigitte Thomas; **16** Marijke Heuff (designer Mien Ruys, Dedemsvaart); **17** Georges Lévêque; **18** above left Lamontagne; **18** above right Georges Lévêque; **18** center left Ron Sutherland/Garden Picture Library; **18** center right Gary Rogers; **18** below left Brigitte Thomas; **18** below right Ron Sutherland/Garden Picture Library; **19** above left Brigitte Thomas; **19** above right Steven Wooster/Garden Picture Library; **19** center left Anthony Paul/Garden Picture Library; **19** center right Lamontagne; **19** below left Lamontagne; **19** below right Ron Sutherland/Garden Picture Library; **20** above Georges Lévêque; **20** below left Belle (Geoff Lung); **20** below right Georges Lévêque; **21** above Tim Street-Porter/Elizabeth Whiting & Associates; **21** below left Bent Rej; **21** below right Rodney Hyett/Elizabeth Whiting & Associates; **43** Neil Lorimer/ Elizabeth Whiting & Associates; **45** Lars Hallen (M-L Rosenbroijer); **46** left Andrew Payne/Garden Picture Library; **46** center René Stoeltie; **46** right Gary Rogers/ Garden Picture Library; **47** Brigitte Thomas; **48** Lamontagne; **49** left Gillian Darley/Edifice; **49** right S & O Mathews; **50** left Marijke Heuff (designer K Noordhuis); **50** center Andrew Lawson; **50** right Brigitte Thomas; **51** above Oliver Gregory; **51** below left Andrew Lawson; **51** below right Marijke Heuff (Mr & Mrs Brinkworth); **70** Boys Syndication; **74** Marijke Heuff (Mr F Tiebout and Mr F de Greeuw); **76** Marijke Heuff (Mr & Mrs Adriaanse-Quint); **78** left Brigitte Thomas; **78** center Lamontagne; **78** right Brigitte Thomas; **79** Ron Sutherland/Garden Picture Library; **80** Nexus Designs, Melbourne, Australia; **81** above left Christian Sarramon; **81** above right Lamontagne; **81** below Georges Lévêque; **82** above Hugh Palmer; **82** below left Ron Sutherland/Garden Picture Library (designer Murray Collins); **82** below right Lamontange; **83** above Brigitte Thomas; **83** below left Eric Crichton; **83** below right Lamontagne; **94** Lamontagne; **96** left Joanne Pavia/Garden Picture Library; **96** center Brigitte Thomas; **96** right Brigitte Thomas; **97** Hugh Palmer; **98** above Brigitte Thomas; **98** center Lamontagne; **98** below Georges Lévêque; **99** Hugh Palmer; **100** above left Georges Lévêque; **100** above right Philippa Lewis/Ediface; **100** center left Lamontagne; **100** center right Marijke Heuff; **100** below left Lamontagne; **100** below right Houses & Interiors; **101** above left Brigitte Thomas; **101** above right Philippa Lewis/Ediface; **101** center left Philippa Lewis/Ediface; **101** center right Gary Chowanetz/Elizabeth Whiting & Associates; **101** below left Ron Sutherland/Garden Picture Library; **101** below right Gary Chowanetz/ Elizabeth Whiting & Associates; **102** left Hugh Palmer; **102** right Georges Lévêque; **103** above Brigitte Thomas; **103** below Gilles de Chabaneix for Terence Conran; **124** left Lamontagne; **124** center Georges Lévêque; **124** right Lamontagne; **125** Georges Lévêque; **126** left Jerry Harpur/Elizabeth Whiting & Associates; **126** right Gary Rogers/Garden Picture Library; **127** Brigitte Thomas; **128** Jerry Harpur/ Elizabeth Whiting & Associates (designed by Clifton Nurseries); **129** above Eric Crichton; **129** below left S & O Mathews; **129** below right Georges Lévêque.

The following photographs were specially taken for Conran Octopus by **Nadia Mackenzie**:
1–7, 23–39, 53–69, 85–92, 105–121, 131–139.